Photo credits:
Cover: Top (l-r): *Photography by Emily Gilbert; Warren Jagger Photography;*
   From House to Home/Jonathan Harper, Eric Roth
   Lower: *Linda Williamson Photography*
Spine: *Photogrpahy by Emily Gilbert*
Front endsheet: *Warren Jagger Photography*
Back endsheet: *Dan Muro, fastforwardunlimited*
Title page: *Thomas McConnell@mconnellphoto.net*
Contents page: *D. Peter Hurd*

Other Schiffer Books on Related Subjects:

Schiffer Books are available at special discounts for bulk purchases for sales promotions or premiums. Special editions, including personalized covers, corporate imprints, and excerpts can be created in large quantities for special needs. For more information contact the publisher:

Published by Schiffer Publishing Ltd.
4880 Lower Valley Road
Atglen, PA 19310
Phone: (610) 593-1777; Fax: (610) 593-2002
E-mail: Info@schifferbooks.com

For the largest selection of fine reference books on this and related subjects, please visit our web site at **www.schifferbooks.com**
We are always looking for people to write books on new and related subjects. If you have an idea for a book please contact us at the above address.

This book may be purchased from the publisher.
Include $5.00 for shipping.
Please try your bookstore first.
You may write for a free catalog.

In Europe, Schiffer books are distributed by
Bushwood Books
6 Marksbury Ave.
Kew Gardens
Surrey TW9 4JF England
Phone: 44 (0) 20 8392 8585; Fax: 44 (0) 20 8392 9876
E-mail: info@bushwoodbooks.co.uk
Website: www.bushwoodbooks.co.uk

SHORE DÉCOR
Design at the Water's Edge

E. Ashley Rooney

With Andreas Charalambous

Schiffer Publishing Ltd®

4880 Lower Valley Road Atglen, Pennsylvania 19310

CONTENTS

Acknowledgments

Barbara Purchia makes this work possible. My husband, D. Peter Lund, makes it fun, and Tricia Traxler, an inspired decorator herself, gave me some good leads.

Courtesy of Eleanor Lund

4

Foreword: The Shore

Andreas Charalambous

shore. *Noun—the land along the edge of a sea, lake, river or other large body of water*

The word itself evokes memories of one's youth by the beach, a lake, a river, or a pond...carefree. Where land and water meet—the tenuous ever-changing border between them is a magnet for our minds every time we need to escape the mundane. Whether it's the sound of the waves, the vision of a blue, aqua, or turquoise reflection of the water, or a sublime feeling at dusk or dawn, most of us have memories of a shoreline. Hence, the almost universal attraction to and appeal of places on the shore for all year living, a weekend getaway, or a summer escape.

I have had the opportunity from time to time to design homes on the shore both for clients and for myself. Two of them are featured in this book: a house for a young couple on the Potomac River, south of Washington, D.C., and my own apartment on Biscayne Bay in South Beach. The approach and inspiration of each vary as much as the view! Ultimately, what makes these homes unique is the blend of the same parameters that make for *any* successful and memorable project: who the client is; what their lifestyle is all about; the specifics of the home itself — the location, size, views, structure, finishes; and an inspiration that can blend all these together to create the one-of-a kind solution, marrying all these elements into a successful whole that looks good and works well!

In the House by the River (p.100) we opened the home to the views. We made the old sliding doors to the balcony into a series of French doors with glass panels that enlarge the overall exposure to and view of the water. Wherever window coverings were required for privacy or regulating the hot sun, we used shades that, even when they are down, still allow for a controlled view to the outside. We used railings throughout, inspired by a ship rail; created playful, round cut-outs in the bathroom privacy film inspired from water bubbles; and used lighting, finishes, and colors that create an ever-changing, uncluttered, modern yet warm environment that makes the home all about the view.

In the South Beach retreat (p.124), the blue of the water was the inspiration throughout. Everything else was white: the wide porcelain floors, white walls, white furniture (with different finishes and textures), that don't compete for attention with the views of Biscayne Bay and the skyline of Miami seen from the windows facing West, and the Atlantic Ocean seen from the north wall of windows. The view outside and the nautical-inspired artwork and accessories are the only splashes of color. The blue LED light behind the paneled wall in the living room transforms the space into a *Zen* lounge at sundown; the breeze makes the Twiggy floor lamp in the living room move as if alive; and, lest you turn your back to the view for a second (almost impossible), the pebbles in the bathroom floor and wall remind you of the beaches that lie below.

A home on the water's edge or shore is an opportunity to invite the view outside the window to become the inspiration for what transpires within. The challenge is attempting to dissolve the border between the inside and outside world and to use that as the catalyst in making the appropriate moves, be it in the architecture, the interiors, the furniture selection, the fabrics, the lighting, the mood — thus making the home uniquely a "place on the shore" — for being there means becoming one with the water. In the following book, you will find many elegant homes that do that.

Andreas Charalambous, AIA, IIDA, Principal of FORMA Design, combines over twenty years of experience in architecture and interior architecture with his deep interest in all aspects of design and a career in painting and photography.

Introduction
Homes on the Water's Edge

I grew up on Long Island Sound in an area of rivers, ponds, and brooks. Like many children, I played in the brooks, damming them, sending small boats down them, looking for fish and waterbugs, dropping pebbles in the water, and watching the ripples circling on and on.

There is something wonderful about living on the water's edge.

Many of us dream about having a house there. Some want the uncertainty of living at the ocean's edge. Others want the gentle lapping of a lake; some want the gurgle of a stream or the babble of the brook.

The United States certainly has many beautiful waterfront sites. They range from our rivers and the many lakes, to the ponds, brooks, and oceans. The early settlers and Native Americans looked to these for sustenance and water. Today, many of these sites are seen as tourist attractions. They are found alongside quaint villages with mom-and-pop restaurants, upscale boutiques, and scenic drives. Some can be found within urban settings, rich with cultural activities and recreational challenges. Still others can be found among deep forests, open meadows, and great cliffs.

Courtesy of Linda Williamson

This book presents many homes that sit on the water's edge. They range from classic to contemporary, from casually elegant to serenely traditional. Their designers describe them, so you can visualize them through the designer's eyes and the camera. Many homeowners mention the beauty of living on the water: from the first tender, green days of spring, when pastel blooms paint the hills, to those warm June days, when boats of all sizes and types fill the waterways, to the cool crisp days of fall, when the land blazes red, gold, and orange. When winter comes and snowflakes fall into the murmuring water, life on the water changes. People leave, and the land becomes quiet again with only the snapping, crackling ice punctuating the cold. New animals appear, and the chimney smoke settles into the valleys.

Most owners of waterfront homes study, love, and feel close to nature. They mention the joys of watching the loons, the ospreys, the herons, the ducks, the deer, the fox, and even the seals. Living on the water, beyond the confusion of life, can bring us into rhythm with nature. It helps us know where we belong. It restores us — and makes us feel whole again.

Our houses on the water's edge can be modest or opulent, simple or complex, open or closed. They need to relate to and not be overpowered by the water. They need to stand up to the power of the water and the wind — to respect the richness of life on the water without overwhelming or hiding it. The intent of this book is to allow you to dream about your own home on the water's edge.

Homes on the water are a dream for many of us. They respond to our need for recreation and respite, revitalization and refuge. English and French royalty had country homes where they would retire for recreation and rest. During the Golden Age of the nineteenth century, millionaires in the United States built great summer cottages in Newport, Rhode Island, where they could retire in unabashed opulence for six weeks during the heat of the summer. Others built in upstate New York, coastal Maine, and Florida, of course.

Courtesy of D. Peter Lund

Courtesy of D. Peter Lund

Courtesy of D. Peter Lund

Investing in a Vacation-to-Retirement Home

Many homes on the water's edge are vacation-to-retirement homes. According to the experts, today's popular spots include:

Cape Cod, Massachusetts
Brigantine Island, New Jersey
Island Beach, New Jersey
Cape May, New Jersey
Boca Raton, Florida (Palm Beach County)
Gulf Coast, Florida
Jupiter Island, Florida
Punta Gorda, Florida
Sanibel Island, Florida
Naples, Florida
Lake Tahoe, California (El Dorado County)

Some buy a waterfront home as an investment in the future — a possible place for retirement. The concept of buying or building a vacation-to-retirement home sparks our imaginations and allows us to dream of escaping our normal humdrum existence. We see this home as the central gathering place, where a far-flung clan can meet for vacations and enjoy fun, friends, and some time on the golf course. We see it as a place where we can write in our journals, find spiritual solace, and walk in piney forests or maybe hear the uplifting symphony. Owning a vacation-to-retirement home allows us to tap into visions of a worry-free life of water activities (or mountain or golf activities) — a life filled with joy and leisure. It is a place for families to share time together and create memories for their children and grandchildren.

Many see their (potential) waterfront area as an investment with significant appreciation potential. That simple little cabin along the bay can be one of the best ways to build wealth while providing life-long fun for you and your family. After all, investing in real estate has been, historically, one of the best ways to develop capital.

During the past decade, second home ownership has jumped significantly. The Housing Vacancy Survey put the growth in second homes between 1995 and 2005 at 22 percent — a 1.2 million increase in just ten years (Joint Center for Housing Studies of Harvard University). Motivated by those same factors, along with the desire to retire in multiple locations, more people are picking up third homes, too. Researchers believe that the demand for second homes is about to burgeon, as 40 million baby boomers reach prime second-home-buying age.

Waterfront property offers a range of investment opportunities. The National Association of Homebuilders reports that a body of water within 300 feet increases a home's value by nearly one-third (Emrath, P., 2004). Our lakes, oceans, rivers are limited resources, so property on or near these recreational areas is likely to gain in value. As the numbers of high-income, high-asset, middle-age or older couples, who have children nearing adulthood or have no children living at home, decide to purchase that vacation-to-retirement home, that cute coastal town or that charming lake community will be even more desirable.

Courtesy of D. Peter Lund

12

Finding the Right Home

A home on the water can be a cabin or a palace, a condo or a mobile home. To find the right one, you need to define whom you are while on vacation and the type of lifestyle that you desire during that time — and once you are retired.

Perhaps you are the avid fisherman, who wants to live and breathe for that fish, or maybe you prefer visiting the local museums and listening to the symphony or want to snowshoe in peaceful tranquility. Or maybe you just want the sound of the wind on the water and a roaring fire.

In contemplating the purchase or construction of a vacation-to-retirement home, you need to analyze your primary reasons for undertaking this step.

• What is your ideal travel distance? Is a 4-hour drive too long for a weekend? Distance is also an important consideration if you are planning on hosting friends and family. People are not always willing to travel long distances — especially for a brief weekend. If you will only have time to visit your new home a few weeks a year before you retire, a timeshare or rental may be more cost-effective and easier to maintain.

• If you are just buying a vacation home, ask yourself what are your most enjoyable vacation experiences? What activities do you enjoy the most? Are those activities available? How frequently will you visit it?

• If you considering ultimately retiring there, you probably should consider what your needs may be as you mature. For example, you may not care now, but ultimately you may want your master bedroom and laundry on the main floor. Older knees don't always like that climb up the stairs!

• If you are considering making this your permanent residence, check it out thoroughly. Talk to other property owners, investigate municipal and property taxes, access to health care and home/auto services, noise and parking problems during the tourist season, and the availability of recreational/cultural facilities, restaurants, and shopping.

Experts suggest renting before buying in an unfamiliar area to help determine if this is the place for you. I met a couple who moved to Boston for three months to check it out as a possible vacation-to-retirement spot. They wanted to determine for themselves whether it was as vibrant a community as the ads said.

• What do you want in the way of services? Many people buy condos or homes in an association because they won't have to worry about maintenance. Others prefer taking care of their own necessities, doing their own work. The question you need to ask is what will happen if you should become incapacitated later on. Are the interior doorways wide enough for a wheelchair?

If you are considering a vacation-to retirement home, you should consider whether the house provides easy living for all ages and abilities: one-story living, wide halls, baths, and doorways, and no-step entries can make life simpler when your needs change.

• Can you handle the tax implications and financing? Mortgage interest and property taxes on a second home may be tax deductible (depending upon the use you make of it), just as are the interest payments on the mortgage for your primary home. Tax laws are complicated and constantly change. Be sure to consult your professional tax advisor.

There are also those hidden costs such as homeowner's insurance, taxes, maintenance costs, security to protect the home while you're gone, and travel expenses. And just like your primary residence, you'll pay for services such as sewer, water, electricity/gas, and phone. You may also need to consider unusual costs, such as winterizing a cabin on the lakefront or adding an alarm system.

Courtesy of D. Peter Lund

A vacation home can offer a break from the stresses of everyday life, giving us an opportunity to recharge, relax, and gain perspective. A vacation-to retirement home can provide us with a permanent place to spend alone or with family and friends—a time to pay attention to all the people and interests that get forgotten in our dot-com worlds.

Creating Your Own Special Place

Paging through this book, you will realize that finding a talented designer is the next step in the process of creating a home. Architects, builders, and designers assist people in making dreams come true — whether it is reveling in a peaceful vacation in a lakeside cabin, waterskiing off your own dock, or enjoying your retirement in a new area.

There is no "right" style for a waterfront home. The only style is that which suits you.

This book will offer you a sampling of the variety of houses on the water's edge that you can use as a basis for designing your dream house.

Courtesy of Robert Evans

Courtesy of D. Peter Lund

I.
Casual Elegance

Primavera Residence

JBD conceptualized this grand dining salon after a pavilion, bringing the outside porch setting into the architectural details in the room. Benjamin Moore color Seafoam is used inside the ceiling coffers to create the feeling of sky overhead. An Asmara carpet anchors custom furnishings from Century and Drexel Heritage. Artifacts in the room include hand-blown glass orbs that bring ocean color into the space. The rich walnut floors are from Carlisle Flooring. *Photography by Warren Jagger Photography*

Although not the architect of this house, Judd Brown Designs' (JBD) role expanded early on to provide details and refinements to the recently constructed home. Towering fireplaces with chimney pots and exterior woodwork reflecting coastal motifs were used to define local artisan leaded glass windows. Holidaze Stained Glass provided the leaded glass. *Photography by Warren Jagger Photography*

A custom banquette provides a cozy setting for the family to enjoy panoramic views while dining. The sea grass green flannel fabric on the banquette compliments the color-tone of the walls above the beadboard. The bronze light fixture above the table is by Vaughan Lighting. The chair by Woodbridge Furniture is custom painted green. *Photography by Warren Jagger Photography*

What can be better than enjoying a glass of wine overlooking the ocean on a beautiful summer day in Rhode Island? A custom designed mahogany handrail with stainless steel dowels tops the stonework of the upper ocean deck. Gaslights from McLean Lighting add an element of jewelry to the stairway. *Photography by Warren Jagger Photography*

A custom banquette provides a cozy setting for the family to enjoy panoramic views while dining. The sea grass green flannel fabric on the banquette compliments the color-tone of the walls above the beadboard. The bronze light fixture above the table is by Vaughan Lighting. The chair by Woodbridge Furniture is custom painted green. *Photography by Warren Jagger Photography*

Every seaside home should have a daybed under the ocean sky. JBD carefully selected upholstery to play off the color of the landscape above for this dramatic setting. The designers created niches for candles in the stonewall. A fireplace turns the space into a relaxing lounge area where guests listen to the waves crashing below. The exterior furniture is by Gloster. *Photography by Warren Jagger Photography*

Off the dining room is an elegant seaside porch with antique wicker furniture upholstered in classic blue and white fabrics. The designers created a custom exterior lantern with seeded glass that hangs from a cathedral ceiling painted in Benjamin Moore Seafoam. Upholstered chaise lounges provide unobstructed views on a clear day with antique porcelain garden stools to rest a chilled drink. *Photography by Warren Jagger Photography*

Appearing like a vignette from a sea captain's home, a custom William Spitzmiller lamp in mercury glass is flanked by two sophisticated Ralph Lauren spindle chairs upholstered in fine linen by Pierre Frey and Schumacher. In the foreground, a Ficks Reed game table in a tortoise shell finish provides a comfortable setting. Custom drapery and motorized shades provide an instant closure to the room when necessary for television viewing. *Photography by Warren Jagger Photography*

Waking up to the morning sun in this light-filled bedroom with the custom iron and crystal chandelier in the cupola creates a feeling of elegance rivaling a New England coastal inn. The Solomon Brothers upholstered bed is dressed in handmade silk bedding by Mario and Marielena executed by the designers using a color palette of seafoam green, ivory, and celery. An intimate seating area provides spectacular views of the ocean and landscape across the bay. *Photography by Warren Jagger Photography*

One of the family's three daughters enjoys a wonderful opportunity to curl up in this tufted, plaid lounge chair to read her favorite book or simply to enjoy the view of the water. *Photography by Warren Jagger Photography*

This lower level bedroom created a challenge that the designers embraced using bold, stunning blue paint in a high gloss finish by Benjamin Moore, as a background to white ceramic lamps and crisp bedding. The designers created lacquered shadow boxes with coral silk backing to display seashells that find balance in the coral throw pillow and mohair throw on the chaise at the foot of the bed. The oil painting reflects the seaside ambiance that the family enjoys. *Photography by Warren Jagger Photography*

Art-Filled Contemporary

"The Bather," a bronze sculpture by Texas artist Charles Strain, greets visitors to a Pacific Northwest home remodeled to showcase an extensive art collection. Designer Molly McIntosh, Gracious Living Interior Design, used soft earth-toned colors, textural fabrics, and comfortable furnishings to warm the large, open interiors and tie together an extensive collection of glass, paintings, sculpture, rugs, and handcrafted furniture. In a climate famous for temperate yet extended periods of gray, Northwesterners take advantage of energy-efficient materials to surround themselves with windows—the better to appreciate the endlessly changing vistas fashioned by Mother Nature. Located on Fidalgo Island, the closest and bridge-linked beginning of the famed San Juan Islands, the home's southwesterly orientation brings light streaming into the home year-round. Seaform-like, ball-and-tendril chandeliers by Marty White Elk punctuate the entry and living room and sitting area. *Courtesy of www.kp-studios.com*

The 1980s home, once dominated by mirror-covered walls, has been re-imagined as a minimalist setting for a spectacular collection of art glass. Playing off existing marble foyer flooring, McIntosh's recommendation of cream with a tint of apricot successfully replaced the owner's original paint choice, which turned out far too pink. The new soft hue establishes a warm, comfortable, low-key backdrop for simply styled furnishings and an extensive display of art. *Courtesy of www. kp-studios.com*

Overlooking Allan and Burrows islands — part of the San Juan Island archipelago, the room benefits from reflected year-round light, dancing off a succession of intriguing shapes and materials. Seating was placed in the center of the large open room to allow more space for three settees — matching Thomas Moser pieces and an armless Stickley sofa that echoes similar curvaceous lines. Fabrics in a range of toast, pumpkin, and caramel complement the abundant warm cherry wood tones, flattering without distracting from the craftsmanship and art. The grand piano commands a primo site in the room's 20-foot-high curved bay. To lower the towering ceilings to a more human scale as well as inject some softened surfaces, McIntosh worked with the owners, who used craftsman Andrew Valley of Bow, Washington, to design narrow, eight-foot-tall, clean-lined bookcases and create a focal point across from the sitting area. By filling the shelves with books rather than the usual mix of books and accessories, McIntosh sought to quiet the pieces visually so as not to compete with other elements throughout the room. Cocktail table sculpture — and ever-changing prism — is "The Embryo" by Jiyong Lee. *Courtesy of www.kp-studios.com*

The fireplace's outdated styling was eliminated and surfaces simplified to create a flattering backdrop for art. Once mirror-clad walls have been resurfaced in natural, subtly mottled limestone. Within the fireplace—which opens on two sides to the living room and dining area—gas flames ripple across a bed of polished stones from jets below. Adjacent to the fireplace, the wall was pierced to allow light and views to flow between rooms as well as create a protected, cherry-trimmed alcove where special pieces of glass are showcased on top-lit glass shelves. *Courtesy of www.kp-studios.com*

A playfully off-kilter curio cabinet adds an updated twist to the simply styled dining room table and shapely slat-back chairs by Harden. The owner, an accomplished amateur woodworker in his own right, crafted the table, with leaves that retract beneath the top and a softly rounded skirt to protect clothing. Mismatched dishes continue the home's eclectic spirit. The sunny nook is used for both formal and everyday dining, with views that extend both to the water and the side deck and garden. *Courtesy of www.kp-studios.com*

McIntosh created an inviting sitting area anchored by a pair of sink-into chairs and an ottoman in rich saddle leather to fill a void between kitchen and dining room, where another table would have been redundant. Handsome from all angles, the seating is movable to suit the occasion, and has proved a popular spot for guests or spouse to keep the cook in the adjacent kitchen company. *Courtesy of www. kp-studios.com*

Nestled amidst custom Shaker-style cherry cabinets, a chef-worthy Wolf stove and space-age hood add up to a dramatic kitchen focal point—and the source of someone's favorite chocolate chip cookies. The owner loves the mottled gold, black, and salmon-toned "Juparana Bordeaux" granite countertop for its fingerprint- and dust-masking properties. The granite backsplash makes cleanup a cinch.

Separating the living and eating areas, a custom made console with simple Shaker styling serves as both room divider and super-functional bar, server, and close-at-hand storage for glassware, dishes, and linens. The serviceable "Beaujolais nouveau" granite top echoes materials in the adjacent kitchen. *Courtesy of www.kp-studios.com*

A silk bed skirt adds a touch of upscale flare to custom bedding. An existing Harden bed anchors an assemblage of handcrafted furnishings, including a rocker by Thomas Far and bench by Peggy Hume Hudson. Designer McIntosh suggested the woven shades for texture and to temper the abundant light—even during the Northwest's notorious winters, when the landscape often resembles an Edward Weston photo with every conceivable shade of gray. Throughout the home, the owners' collection of oriental rugs grounds the home's spontaneous, eclectic look with a touch of history. *Courtesy of www.kp-studios.com*

New Seaside Shingle

Kingsley Belcher Knauss, ASID of KBK Interior Design, added millwork details and architectural elements to create a classic beach house with the casual elegance that the client desired. Minutes from Manhattan, this newly constructed seaside shingle style home transports these city dwellers to the relaxed atmosphere of a weekend retreat but with all the conveniences of a "primary residence." Sea glass was the inspiration for the aqua, pear green, and chocolate color palette. Hand-blocked floral cotton window treatments hang from hand forged iron hardware in the great room. Cobalt blue and white canisters add a touch of deep blue without going "overboard." Woven textures on upholstery pieces add an earthiness and warmth with natural linen and chocolate herringbone fabric on the deep sofas and accent woven linens of pear and blue check on smaller pieces. Painted wainscot, coffered ceilings with beadboard planking, and hand crafted Poseidon ceramic tile at the fireplace are some of the details reinforcing architectural elements of years gone by. *Courtesy of Paul S. Bartholomew, ABIPP*

Oversized French lounge chairs with distressed pear green frames and down-blend check cushions are a blue green palette reminiscent of sea glass. These colors then transition into the adjoining breakfast room and kitchen. *Courtesy of Paul S. Bartholomew, ABIPP*

This large great room is softened by the full length floral cotton panels with hand sewn pinch-pleated detailing that hang from a square twist hand-forged iron rod with natural pewter finish. Decorative pillows with inset geometric accent fabrics of squares and triangles add a sense of playfulness to the room, making it more inviting. *Courtesy of Paul S. Bartholomew, ABIPP*

The great room is a multi-purpose room for storing games, watching television, or sitting peacefully by the fire with a good book. KBK tucked storage into spaces defined by arched walkways to the foyer and kitchen. By painting these cabinets the trim color, they became part of the architectural detailing of the room, along with the wainscot and beadboard coffered ceiling. *Courtesy of Paul S. Bartholomew, ABIPP*

This dining space has a pass-through from the kitchen, great room, and a view of a backyard garden. The mix of formal window treatment with casual fabrics makes for light and airy dining. The large cobalt damask print over aqua reinforces the color scheme of the great room. The multi-blue check from the great room reappears as seat cushions and dresses down the formality of the tasseled trimmed linen drapery. *Courtesy of Paul S. Bartholomew, ABIPP*

The backsplash with its sea glass blue, green, and amber offsets the ivory paint of bench-made cabinets. The cabinets have a beaded inset frame with recessed panel doors, seedy glass, and a "furniture-style" base hiding the typical recessed toe kicks. The distressed knotty pine island provides a smooth transition between the work and entertaining spaces, keeping guests from being underfoot. The millwork detail, beadboard ceiling, and column openings give this small kitchen a big feel. *Courtesy of Paul S. Bartholomew, ABIPP*

This bathroom is all about layering of earth tones and texture. The basket weave tumbled limestone floor pattern with inlay mocha glass tile provides great variations in texture. The mocha glass is again seen in the wall border and as an accent feature on the custom sink with glass tile and ceramic seashells. KBK coordinated the weathered brass faucets with the cabinet hardware, silver gilt iron sconces, and decorative mirror. The window treatment of taupe linen sheer and mocha glass beads reinforces the varied textures throughout this space. *Courtesy of Paul S. Bartholomew, ABIPP*

The master bedroom is small, but cozy with a four-poster iron bed with aqua and white embroidered drapery providing intimacy to the space. A linen upholstered settee adds a soft touch and comfortable spot to tie shoes. An arched opening provides the pass through to the unique master closet that is more of a specialty room than closet. *Courtesy of Paul S. Bartholomew, ABIPP*

Because of the layout of the house, one has to pass through the closet to get to the master bathroom. This detail provided numerous challenges in how to minimize the mess and clutter of a room typically left out of view. KBK created custom "trellis" doors with aqua plaid privacy panels to hide the hanging clothing while providing color and interest. His and her dressers contained cloth-lined drawers for jewelry, hats, and smaller clothing articles. White-painted shelving runs up to the ceiling crown and over windows to provide the most storage possible.

Ming green and limestone Greek Wave inlay tile floor pattern organizes this space, while the celadon green hand made wall tile offers a calming environment to relax in. A paneled upper wall with niche, bow front vanity, and tub deck, which continues into the shower, provides unexpected detail to this master bathroom. *Courtesy of Paul S. Bartholomew, ABIPP*

The scalloped bed drapery in lime green and blue with milk glass drapery holdbacks makes this little girl's room special. The scallop and curves reoccur in the painted antique side table, mirror, and custom headboard. The more juvenile boat and sea creature cotton prints are left to pillows that will appeal to this 6-year-old, without dating this room as the child grows. *Courtesy of Paul S. Bartholomew, ABIPP*

This private den off of the master bedroom provides a quiet setting for watching television or reading. The walls are paneled in a wide grooved plank in a pale taupe with Tramp art frames featuring antique zoological fish prints adding to the overlying textures within the space. Blue green linen velvet sofas and chocolate and aqua seashell linen fabric provide a serene palette. *Courtesy of Paul S. Bartholomew, ABIPP*

Swedish-Inspired Design

The total neutrality of the living room together with the directionality of the herringbone wood floors helps draw one's attention to the waterfront view. The generous bay front window framed with soft white puddling floor-to-ceiling sheers in the living room keep the room light and airy, true to the Swedish style. Two, large beaded crystal and iron chandeliers bisect the huge vaulted space and help bring it down to a more manageable dimension. Occasional darker neutral accents are used to anchor the space, including a massive walnut eighteenth century Spanish cupboard topped with antique French confit jars, wrought iron architectural pieces, and gilded accessories. *Photo by Emily Gilbert*

Ruth Richards Interiors drew on a soothing color palette of light gray, slate blue, and sand echoing the adjacent waterfront view in Longboat Key, Florida. True to the historic Gustavian Swedish period, this design uses Nordic off-white lymed hardwood floors and uninterrupted uniform soft gray walls as the backdrop that unifies the entire first floor. The minimalist entry contains an antique Swedish center hall table with a delicate antique Continental crystal chandelier suspended from a stenciled tray ceiling. *Photo by Emily Gilbert*

Unexpected treasures including a charming French antique birdcage paired with small collectibles sit on an Italian altar table. A custom skirted sectional sofa covered in linen with a contrasting border tucks nicely into the seating area beneath the sweeping staircase. *Photo by Emily Gilbert*

Soothing neutral hues of nature dictate the decor in the informal dining room. Neoclassical wall brackets supporting transfer ware plates flank an old French wall plaque. Pinecones fill the white glazed porcelain bowl below. *Photo by Emily Gilbert*

A timeless all white kitchen becomes Nordic with the addition of a blue center island, Swedish stools, antique toy horse, and white linen slip covered chairs.

Antique French pressed botanicals hang from chains on both sidewalls to complete this serene space. *Photo by Emily Gilbert*

An authentic Swedish Moro clock can be seen through the arched passageway from the living room.
Photo by Emily Gilbert

The master bedroom is furnished with a new Swedish king bed, painted commodes, chaise, and secretary. The soothing blue and gray floral print allows an uninterrupted view of the water. *Photo by Emily Gilbert*

Custom Gustavian cabinetry in the master closets and bath adds European charm and continuity to the master suite. *Photo by Emily Gilbert* (above and right)

The sandy accent color from the first floor is used predominately in the second floor rooms. Reminiscent of the nearby beach, it is a warm color choice for a second master suite and office. The informal window treatment for the upstairs master bedroom is a coarse linen sand colored print suspended by a nautical rope through grommets and finished with dangling shells. *Photo by Emily Gilbert*

A wavy whimsical floor tile and wall mural of chirping seagulls are fun reminders that it's a vacation get away. *Photo by Emily Gilbert*

A queen walnut four-poster bed fills this small guest bedroom with its 10- foot ceilings. Crisp navy accents nicely offset the cream-colored backdrop and are remarkably rich and handsome against the deep tones of the walnut furniture. The same blue and cream tones are carried into the adjacent guest bathroom in the open vanity with storage below and in the shower border designs done in blue tiles. *Photo by Emily Gilbert*

Rock Cliff

Designed by James D. LaRue Architects, this three-story house rests on a beautiful Lake Austin lot. Set far back from the street, this home hints at its Cape Cod origins while boasting magnificent views of the lake from nearly every room. The East Coast influenced architecture comes to life through the oversized double-hung windows and transoms, varied siding colors and patterns, and muted standing seam metal roof. *Courtesy of Coles Hairston Photography*

The slate terrace outside the living room overlooks the lawn to the lake. The two-story guesthouse to the right is connected to the main house through an open-air breezeway, which also serves as a covered porch for the beautiful wood deck. The L-shaped design allows for all the living areas of the home to overlook and enjoy the lawn and the lake. *Courtesy of Coles Hairston Photography*

This multiple landing staircase has railing detailing that is reminiscent of an East coast lighthouse. The light fixtures also reflect the nautical theme. *Courtesy of Coles Hairston Photography*

The slate path to the house extends across an expansive manicured lawn to a low-walled courtyard. The extended front porch roof of the guesthouse creates a simple, inviting entrance to the home. The entry porch is centered on the "lighthouse" tower beyond; it houses the dining room, music room, and third floor library. *Courtesy of Coles Hairston Photography*

Large corner double-hung windows define this sitting alcove in the lakeside master suite. *Courtesy of Coles Hairston Photography*

The natural flow of the home is immediately revealed when entering the understated foyer. Exterior stone brings the outside into this furnished gallery entrance, which opens to the dining room. The wood floors and beams add a seamless flow between the rooms. *Courtesy of Coles Hairston Photography*

The reclaimed wood beams and the river rock fireplace add a sense of warmth and harmony to a living room. *Courtesy of Coles Hairston Photography*

Granite countertops and natural stone flooring add a warm contrast to the painted millwork throughout this fresh kitchen. A charming window over the farmhouse sink is an essential element in capturing the lush garden view. *Courtesy of Coles Hairston Photography*

Guests may never leave this inviting bedroom, which is serene and sunlit from three sides. The French doors that lead to the front courtyard allow guests to come and go freely. *Courtesy of Coles Hairston Photography*

2.
Traditional

Many of us revel in the idea of a more traditional home. Perhaps it is from perusing the fairy tales of our childhood, where all sorts of wondrous people inhabited lovely homes. Perhaps we feel, like Thoreau, that home life is warm and cheery. Perhaps we just want to downsize, to get away from suburbia or the city, and sit on that porch and rock away. Then there are those homes that offer fine design details and craftsmanship, where their owners can escape from their everyday lives to the golf complex, the tennis court, the waterfront, and the woods... or just to the porch.

Courtesy D. Peter Lund

Courtesy D. Peter Lund

Boston Penthouse

This modern Back Bay penthouse apartment has views of Boston Harbor and the Public Gardens directly below. The client wanted a very formal, traditional decor. tj's at the Sign of the Goose added moldings throughout; Regency-style furniture and rich golden tones unify the look. Dramatic night lighting is provided both by the city of Boston and an Italian chandelier. *Courtesy of W. Garrett Scholes*

The silk wall coverings reflect the opulence of the city's lighting. A breakfast bar separates the dining room and kitchen. A luxurious and practical touch is the custom Regency-style barstools and granite counter the client uses every morning for coffee. *Courtesy of W. Garret Scholes*

A luxurious finish is applied to every surface in this bedroom. Rich, warm-hued textiles work beautifully with the traditional furnishings and cherry parquet floor. A dramatic touch is the subtle gold-on-gold striped wallpaper, turned sideways! *Courtesy of W. Garrett Scholes*

Contemporary Update

Frank Lloyd Wright inspired the design for this contemporary waterfront house, which is built into the hillside, taking advantage of the sloping terrain. The expansive windows allow maximum views of the outdoors. On the right side of the house, the kitchen door opens into a rounded covered area, where the client can leave his small airplane. The client asked Teal Michel to update this contemporary home so to reflect the views of blue skies, lake, and foliage. *Courtesy of Teal Michel ASID*

Teal Michel used a green and blue color scheme and balanced this with golden tones in the rug and the natural maple flooring. The large sectional defines the open space. Since the client uses the room primarily in the evening, its focal point is the custom cabinetry featuring the art pieces and a hidden television. *Courtesy of Teal Michel ASID*

The removal of the interior walls allowed the renovated kitchen to connect with nature. To emphasize this connection, Teal Michel selected a sky blue paint for the walls and ceilings. Walnut base cabinets and stainless steel upper cabinets with etched glass insets add interest to the cabinetry. Seating and pillow fabrics reflect the blue-green color palette of outdoors. *Courtesy of Teal Michel ASID*

With sweeping views of the lake, this alcove with its comfortable chaise longue provides a perfect place for reading or meditating on views of the outdoors. Again, the seating uses blue and greens. During the holiday season, the alcove is transformed by a tall Christmas tree, which can be seen from inside and outdoors. Privacy was not an issue in the house, so window treatments were not added. *Courtesy of Teal Michel ASID*

One of the design challenges was to include some element of the clients' Scottish ancestry. The dining room is adjacent to the alcove. Teal Michel designed the table base to hold the engraved family's coat of arms, which is held in place by a brass frame. The chair fabric is a leafy green pattern reflecting the natural environment. *Courtesy of Teal Michel ASID*

Old World Comfort

New owners of a dated 1990s contemporary in the Pacific Northwest set out to redefine their new abode with a warm, comfortable European feel. Tackling the project room by room over a period of three years, the couple indulged their own talents as well as those of consultants and craftspeople. Having established a traditional architectural theme through custom cabinetry, woodwork, and metal accents, the owners called on designer Molly McIntosh, Gracious Living Interior Design, to source a broad choice of furniture and accessories and give the home a finished, cohesive feel.

Playing off the new traditional look, McIntosh created an intentionally eclectic look that appears to have evolved over the years. (In fact, the owners had sold their previous home fully furnished and were starting from scratch!) For the very-much-lived-in living room, she chose sofas in two different styles (for equal-opportunity movie watching comfort) and a handful of unmatched yet complementary occasional tables. Long, silk drapes, hanging from custom-stained rods with gilded finials, are ruched at the top for added interest and accented with bullion and tassel trim. *Courtesy of www.kp-studios.com*

The powder room captures the home's rich textures and tones. An elegant small mirror stands out against cold stripe-plastered walls above a granite countertop and mosaic stone sink. The rich brown-stained cherry cabinets include open shelves at the bottom for towel storage. *Courtesy of www.kp-studios.com*

A built-in wet bar between the living room and kitchen keeps sink, icemaker, and wine cooler close at hand, plus offers generous storage for entertaining needs. *Courtesy of www. kp-studios.com*

The kitchen was expanded and given an aged look with the help of a previous designer, Cheryl Nunn, CN Designs, working with Stone Age Millworks, Oak Harbor, Washington. Raised panel cabinets and modern wrought iron hardware establish a relaxed old-world feel. Two islands, one with a butcher block top, the other tying back to the kitchen's granite countertops, help accommodate multiple cooks as well as kibitzing guests. A decorative stone mosaic behind the cooktop draws the eye across the room to an artistic focal point. *Courtesy of www.kp-studios.com*

Adjacent to the kitchen, a glass-top pedestal table pairs with leather and woven chairs to create a picturesque casual dining nook. Expansive, greenery-framed water views extend from the San Juan Islands to the Olympic Peninsula. McIntosh designed simple yet elegant rope-accented swags to frame the view and visually warm the space. *Courtesy of www.kp-studios.com*

The utilitarian den serves as a hardworking office, but because it opened to the main hallway, it needed to look good, too. Here, McIntosh used a hand-knotted rug to pull together the room's rich wood tones and forest green plastered walls. The dramatic classic wall unit provides hidden storage shelves behind column doors. *Courtesy of www.kp-studios.com*

In the foyer, McIntosh used accessories to establish a lightly detailed European feel. A carved, gilded rectangular mirror picks up the delicate gold tracery in a beautiful chinoiserie demi-lune chest. A pencil-thin lamp and exquisite shade echo the delicacy of the painted chest. *Courtesy of www.kp-studios.com*

The master bedroom is up a half flight of stairs. A quirky striped table presents a welcoming hint of the surprises that are beyond the wide double doors. The sophisticated soft gold wall color flatters the blues and greens of the panoramic outdoor setting. *Courtesy of www.kp-studios.com*

In the master bedroom, with its tree house feel and panoramic views, the owners wanted to create an intimate seating area around the fireplace using over-sized chairs. McIntosh dressed large-scale seating in textured chenille, accenting the casual look with upscale coppery brown silk on pillows and ottoman. A Seattle firm crafted the decorative fireplace wrought iron screen, along with other metal accents throughout the house. *Courtesy of www.kp-studios.com*

The master bedroom's sculptural platform bed received high-class treatment with custom bedding in dark tones laced with intriguing textures. Eye-catching and versatile benches at the foot of the bed are covered in velvet-appliquéd silk. Embossed silk curtains to warm the generous-sized room and frame the view are trimmed with prism-like glass beads that catch the light of the setting sun. *Courtesy of www.kp-studios.com*

A thorough believer in details making the difference, McIntosh carried European elegance into the spacious master bath, creating a focal point out of its well-appointed corner soaking tub. Swags and cascades of striated silk with loop fringe frame the views of distant tankers, tugs, and yachts, The curtain rod echoes the home's metalwork with a hand-hammered pole and finials that repeat the curvaceous shaping of an adjacent light fixture over the sink. *Courtesy of www.kp-studios.com*

Bay View Grand: Apartment

This view is looking back at the entrance. The mirror reflects the ocean view. The family room sectional and the table chairs are by Oscar de La Renta at Century; the fabric is by Nomi at Summit. *Courtesy of Victor Elias/VPL Photo*

Jerry Jacobs designed this apartment overlooking the bay. This view is from the entrance: the sea and the horizon. The blue walls and lighter blue ceiling reflect the blue water. *Courtesy of Victor Elias/VPL Photo*

The water is reflected in the dining room, family room, and foyer. The ceilings in main rooms were raised for more ample space. *Courtesy of Victor Elias/VPL Photo*

The entrance has a glass console with a Crema Maya column in a trompe l'oeil effect. *Courtesy of Victor Elias/VPL Photo*

Jacobs used mirrors and the ocean views to full advantage in the bedrooms.

To enlarge the guest bedroom so that it could hold two queen-sized beds, Jacobs turned a walk-in closet into a reach-in closet. The lime green walls and sky blue ceiling show off the Williams Sonoma Home linens, tables, and lamp and the West Elm headboards. *Courtesy of Victor Elias/VPL Photo*

Nubble Light Waterfront Home

Here, the open floor plan and unusual lighting fixtures create a wonderful atmosphere for entertaining. Two square tables work together or separately to handle any seating arrangement; plush settees serve as the hosts' seating. An Italian sideboard, a contemporary chandelier, and a strong, simple window treatment framing the dramatic ocean view complete the room. *Courtesy of W. Garrett Scholes*

tj's at the Sign of the Goose created a soothing "transitional" design style for this dramatic home set on a cliff by the Maine coast's historic Nubble Light. Because it was a year-round home, tj's chose furnishings and surface treatments to provide flexibility for multi-season living and entertaining and to create a relaxing and luxurious shelter. *Courtesy of W. Garrett Scholes*

Red lacquer custom cabinetry, black marble, and a mixture of metals (gold leaf, brushed nickel, and bronze) are not only luxurious, but reflect the variable seacoast light. *Courtesy of W. Garrett Scholes*

Northwest Island Home

Designed by Chester Architecture, this Northwest style house is located on an island 12 miles from downtown Seattle. An Asian influence is apparent in the exterior of the house, which features a river rock base and wall shingles. The patios are paved in dark slate, which extends into the entry, kitchen, and dining areas. The roofing is a gray metal, and the exterior trim is charcoal while the singles have a natural stain. The deck railings and beam extensions add an Asian feeling to the home. *Courtesy of Michael A. Moore Photographer*

The house has a panoramic view of the City of Seattle and Puget Sound, a waterway that is active day and night. The designer, Bennett Howard Studios, used a classic "Tone on Tone" approach to the interior design. The basic colors are in the same hue and tone as the bleached and white washed wood paneling and trim. The overall colors are in the beige and platinum ranges. However the designer introduced accents in the furnishings and accessories that use organic color tones and hues that are indigenous to the Pacific Northwest. The tone on tone finishes provide a neutral background for an abundant art and sculpture collection as well as accessories and personal items that reflect the owner's personality. The interior design approach for this project seamlessly combines the owner's desire to have a place for entertaining as well as a comfortable, secure and serene sense of home.
Courtesy of John Keppeler

The stair leading to the entry of the home descends through a shade garden next to a garden/art studio. The exterior features round steel columns that are reminiscent of the many industrial dock and waterfront structures seen on Puget Sound. Protected from the elements by a small second story deck, the steel columns frame the entry. *Courtesy of Michael A. Moore Photographer*

The owners wanted a house that they could entertain in as well as enjoy on quiet days and intimate evenings. To meet those needs, the house has a large entertaining room built around the reconstructed fireplace and a large wet bar, where guest can sit and enjoy conversation and view the water and the city. The living room is sunken so that the view can be seen from the kitchen and dining areas as well as the living room. *Courtesy of Michael A. Moore Photographer*

A white oak circular staircase separates the entertainment room from the dining, kitchen, and living rooms. The stair treads to the living and dining areas are inlaid with a black granite stair runner while the stair treads to the second floor are inlaid with carpet. The second floor of the home features two guest bedrooms, a media room and master bedroom suite. The media room staircase and one of the guest bedrooms are open to the entertainment area on the first floor, which adds to the open floor plan concept of this house. *Courtesy of Michael A. Moore Photographer*

A shoji screen can close off the kitchen from the dining room when serving a formal dinner. The clients also have the choice to enjoy a private meal next to a small fireplace in a breakfast nook off the kitchen with a view to north Puget Sound. *Courtesy of Michael A. Moore Photographer*

The master bedroom suite includes a seating area with a fireplace. The master suite also accommodates an office that is open to the kitchen below and can be separated from the master suite with shoji screens for additional privacy. The master bath is adjacent to a large walk in closet. The closet has a private deck overlooking the entry garden. Each of the guest bedrooms has a private bath suite. *Courtesy of Michael A. Moore Photographer*

Nag's Head House

The client chose a sunny peach tone reminiscent of Charleston's "Rainbow Road" for her Nags Head home. The house is typical of the local vernacular of simple wood structures with white trim and an elevated living floor to take advantages of the views. ©
Thomas Kojcsich

Both the client and Gary Inman, Director of Residential Design for Glavé & Holmes Architect wanted the living area to be crisp and relaxed. The blue and white ticking stripes and the cream and sand linen achieve this goal. The coastal location is referenced but is not overt. Embroidered starfish adorn the dining chairs and the linen valances have sail lacings to remind the owner of her days sailing on the Outer Banks. © *Thomas Kojcsich*

The dining table is a unique solution to the client's desire to relive family picnics on the beach. Virginia metal artist, Maurice Beane, fabricated the table based on the designer's sketch. The table has a virtual beachscape of pure white sand, driftwood, and sea life beneath a crystal clear glass top. Dining at the table gives one the sense of being on the beach. © *Thomas Kojcsich*

The kitchen was given a simple face lift. The darkly stained cabinets were painted and top glazed in a soft cream. The hardwood floors were pickled a soft grey, and the hardware was changed to a nautical pewter. The transformation was completed with hand-blocked linens featuring seashells from an artisan in England. © *Thomas Kojcsich*

This guest room is the client's favorite as it was inspired by her late husband's time at Culver Military Academy. Navy linen with brass buttons is complemented by the red cashmere, which bears the family coat-of-arms of husband and wife. There are also nautical elements which recall the couple's passion for sailing during their nearly four decades of summering on the Outer Banks. © *Thomas Kojcsich*

The owner's master bedroom was designed to be peaceful and cozy. She was particularly fond of the hand-blocked linens and requested that her space be uncluttered. Her interest in the local birdlife is documented in the artwork purchased from the Manteo Christmas Shop. © *Thomas Kojcsich*

A Maine Cottage

Most everyone has a dream of owning a cottage on the Maine Coast. tj's at the Sign of the Goose has created a space that is both intimate and dramatic in a garret. Used by relatives and special guests, the furnishings are inviting with their comfortable proportions and jaw dropping for their quality and finish. One long room makes efficient use of each furniture piece. The sleigh bed, tables, and plump comfortable seating make a living area. An antique, hand finished desk at the entrance is both 'foyer' and furniture. *Courtesy of W. Garrett Scholes*

Bethany Beach

Facing the Atlantic Ocean, this custom Rill Architects-designed Bethany Beach, Delaware, retreat includes multiple decks, with a widow's walk that seamlessly works with the facade. This shingle-style residence offers salt-resistant materials to withstand the punishment of an oceanfront property. *Courtesy of Timothy Bell Photography*

Decks overlooking the water allow owners and visitors to take advantage of the scenery. Indoor-outdoor furnishings and accessories are mainstays in this Delaware home. *Courtesy of Timothy Bell Photography*

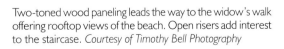

Two-toned wood paneling leads the way to the widow's walk offering rooftop views of the beach. Open risers add interest to the staircase. *Courtesy of Timothy Bell Photography*

Rill Architects created a commercial-grade kitchen, complete with a restaurant-quality range hood, to accommodate large gatherings. Maple cabinets, granite counters, stainless steel appliances, and backsplashes keep the space light and festive. *Courtesy of Timothy Bell Photography*

With unobstructed water views, owners prepare for the day with side mirrors and dual sinks in the owners' suite bathroom. Rill Architects capitalized on this home's great outdoor vistas. *Courtesy of Timothy Bell Photography*

Wood ceilings and walls and tiled flooring stand up to the wear and tear of a beachfront property, including in the banquet-size dining area. There is a strong flow between interior and exterior spaces. *Courtesy of Timothy Bell Photography*

Yacht Club Penthouse

In this penthouse designed by Jacobs Design, Inc., Mexican Morelia region wood columns with fabric are hung on top of the mirror. The mirror reflects the ocean and terrace spa. *Courtesy of Jorge Pablo de Aguinaco*

The tempered glass top breakfast area overlooks the living room. The painting is the Pyramid series by Vicente Rojo. *Courtesy of Jorge Pablo de Aguinaco*

The master bedroom has light pink-to lavender wall, McGuire sofa, linear HVAC diffuser, and antique pair of doors acting as a screen. Mirror at right end shows reflected view. *Courtesy of Jorge Pablo de Aguinaco*

At the landing, there is a glass railing over a built-in bench. The windows have Roman sheer weave shades. *Courtesy of Jorge Pablo de Aguinaco*

Craftsman Style Californian Home

This California Craftsman Style home, designed by Kathy Abell and Terese Moser of Designed Interiors, overlooks the coast of California. Its vantage point, along the bluffs of Del Mar, a community of San Diego, allows the homeowner spectacular views of the surrounding coastlands. The leaded, beveled glass windows display views of the Pacific Ocean through their multi-paned, mahogany frames. *Courtesy of Cogdell Photography*

An antique brass telescope is the focal point of this vignette, creating a nautical feel and an invitation to enjoy the ocean view. European wine jugs and beautifully framed maritime artwork complete the waterfront feel. *Courtesy of Cogdell Photography*

Beautiful, mahogany beams highlight this family room, enhanced by views through traditional Craftsman style windows. Walls of paneled mahogany add warmth to the space. Unique pieces of furniture, upholstered in deep blue and white, invite the family to enjoy the fire and the views of the Pacific. Accent tables are filled with distinctive light fixtures, vintage ginger jars, and priceless family photos. *Courtesy of Cogdell Photography*

In the lower level game room, comfortable, upholstered seating invites a person to linger. The fabric walls create warmth and are a beautiful background for the seafaring artwork. A vintage trunk and distressed wood furniture provide a space to display unique lighting and ocean treasures. *Courtesy of Cogdell Photography*

The raised-hearth fireplace warms the seating area in this seaside guest cottage. The warmth of upholstered furniture pieces, pillows, and throws, soften the room. The arched windows let in plenty of warm sunshine and give the guest beautiful views of the surrounding lush grounds. Large glass containers hold treasures from the sea, and the nautical artwork tie together this charming coastal dwelling. *Courtesy of Cogdell Photography*

Unique blue and white dishes, a fan coral, and starfish are some of the treasures that fill this antique hutch. Set to the side of the main room in the guesthouse, the accessories in the hutch encourage one to explore the tide pools in search of more finds by the seashore. *Courtesy of Cogdell Photography*

Duxbury Harbor

tj's at the Sign of the Goose decorated a cozy two-bedroom Cape style house on the harbor in Duxbury's Powder Point with a major addition in a traditional New England style. New England's warmth is captured in this room with strong red walls and finished ceiling beams. Only 7 by 12 feet, it is a frequent destination for the family. Courtesy *of W. Garrett Scholes*

The dining room has a grand window treatment reflecting the antique buffet table with its Phyfe style table and chairs. The wallpaper is silvery with bird motifs. *Courtesy of W. Garrett Scholes*

This traditionally furnished bedroom directly overlooks the harbor and includes a private veranda. Linen window treatments frame the views. Its pervasive golden color brings warmth — even in the New England winters. *Courtesy of W. Garrett Scholes*

Newport Residence

The combination of the unusual antique bench and the playful contemporary beach scene painting, by noted Newport artist, Henry Finn, gives the entrance lots of style and personality! The design theme throughout the house is this eclectic combination of old world items of grandness, mixed with newer, contemporary elegant furnishings. *Courtesy of D. Reefe*

The living room seating is clustered around the fireplace, which gives the room an intimacy, although it is large and open to the kitchen and other living areas. The custom Tibetan rug by Tufenkian sets the soft leaf-green color palette for the entire area. *Courtesy of D. Reefe*

Between the living room and the kitchen is the perfect sitting area for entertaining. The custom circular rug, by Glen Eden, and the scooped back chairs and round table nicely soften the square space. The yacht model gives homage to the legendary grandness of Newport. *Courtesy of D. Reefe*

The kitchen and dining area with its mahogany wood floor suits this high-end luxury space. The scooped back chairs and round table nicely soften the square shapes of the kitchen and living room. *Courtesy of D. Reefe*

The master bedroom, with large French doors overlooking the harbor, is cozy yet spacious. The corner has luxurious upholstered chairs, with a table between and a desk along side. The color palette is an inviting soft aqua; the wool rug, wall color, and fabrics all stay within the same close range of pale aqua. The artwork throughout the room is a series of sky-water abstract watercolor paintings, in tones that define the lightness and dreamy mood of the room. *Courtesy of D. Reefe*

3.
Contemporary

"Form follows function — that has been misunderstood. Form and function
should be one, joined in a spiritual union. " Frank Lloyd Wright

Courtesy of Eleanor Lund

85

Miami Beach Townhouse

This beautiful holiday townhouse is located on the southernmost tip of Miami Beach. Nearly 4000 square feet are divided among four floors, pool patio, and a roof deck. The house marries relaxing Miami Beach style with New York chic — the city of the client's primary residence. Magdalena Keck Interior Design designed the house with nature-inspired comfort and effortless luxury in mind. She used very few materials, selecting them with great care for their color, texture, and feel in the warm weather. She consistently used coral stone, silk, linen, and wood. Off the living room is a comfortable patio with a plunge pool. The soft white lounge pieces and a huge Royal Botania umbrella complement the teak and stainless steel dining table and chairs. The accessories at the pool patio add a finished look and provide comfort. *Courtesy of Jeff Cate*

The walls throughout the entire house are painted in a warm white Farrow and Ball color called Pointing, which also unifies all living spaces. The focal point of the living room is the "Close" rug by Christopher Farr in soothing tones of pale light blue, cream, and nude. Oversized, four feet deep Flexform sofas are upholstered in a neutral beige / blue linen. A David Weeks four-tier chandelier is comfortably hanging in the double story space, its color perfectly matching the walls. *Courtesy of Jeff Cate*

The coral stone, which is used for all floors, provides cool surfaces and unifies the open kitchen and its espresso stained wood storage with the living area. The island top extends, creating a breakfast surface. The adjustable bar stools in polished chrome are upholstered in dark brown linen. *Courtesy of Jeff Cate*

The light tones of the house contrast with the espresso stained wood throughout. Floating shelves with wood backdrop in the same finish provide ample space for books and art objects. *Courtesy of Jeff Cate*

The upper level of the residence houses the minimalist master bedroom with the grand Nakashima bed and an open bath area. A soft hand tufted silk rug complements the cool coral stone floor. A sculpted wooden Boffi fan hangs above the bed. The David Weeks sconces correspond with the living room chandelier.
Courtesy of Jeff Cate

The open bath area with organically shaped free standing tub and a huge mirror add to the luxury of the master bedroom.
Courtesy of Jeff Cate

The top floor offers the best views of the Atlantic Ocean. It has a small kitchen, a bathroom, a roof deck with a bar and lounge bed, as well as an outdoor television. *Courtesy of Jeff Cate*

Sapphire Towers

This beachfront loft located in downtown San Diego, California, overlooking San Diego Harbor is a great example of an upscale contemporary design scheme undertaken by Ami Samuel Interiors. *Courtesy of Ami Samuel Interiors*

The master bedroom with its contemporary furniture, unique lighting, and calming color scheme gives the client the feeling of a beachfront resort. The wall mirrors expand the space. *Courtesy of Ami Samuel Interiors*

The use of crisp white with a neutral color palette and with fuchsia accent colors, exquisite lighting, and accessories transform this great room into a sophisticated space. *Courtesy of Ami Samuel Interiors*

Steps to the Ocean

Bathed in the light from the ocean, this Truro, Massachusetts, house is designed by Eleven Interiors. The generously sized buttery leather Italian sofa sectional unit is upholstered in durable microsuede, which can take a beating from guests in wet bathing suits. The vibrant painting by Cape Cod artist Elaine Souda hanging above the cozy Italian sandstone fireplace grounds the living room. *Photo © Eric Roth*

Light and airy, this modern dining room designed by Eleven Interiors features three glowing pendants over the table custom designed by Eleven Interiors and built by Studio Fkia in South Boston. Seating expands from 12 to 24 once the extra section is added to the table to ensure entertaining a large crowd is a breeze. One wall of the room is fabricated almost completely of glass with a walkout to the deck. *Photo © Eric Roth*

An open and bright kitchen is made to order from the firm Zeroenergy Design. Its high cantilevered ceiling boasts three square pendant lights, suspended almost transparently over the expansive island finished in bamboo to match the floors. A built-in wall of shelving sheathed in frosted glass meets the storage needs resulting from the lack of overhead cabinets. *Photo © Eric Roth*

A platform king bed and sliding glass doors to a private mahogany deck, which is just steps from the ocean, share the spotlight in the master bedroom. The padded custom triple ottoman at the foot of the bed offers comfort as well as extra seating options. *Photo © Eric Roth*

Creatively using every inch of space in the bathroom, the custom bamboo cabinets are wall mounted, clean, and uncluttered, offering open shelving for towels. The organically shaped bowl sink has a wall-mounted faucet. *Photo © Eric Roth*

Hurst Hollow

This lakeside property designed by Webber + Studio responds to flood plain rules requiring 20-foot stilts for new construction. Neighbors opted for siting a traditional home on wood or concrete cinder blocks to meet the required height. Local boat sheds along the lake inspired this building's industrial aesthetic. *Thomas McConnell@mconnellphoto.net*

Inspired by the systematic approach in pre-manufactured rigid frame technology, the steel frame supports the home. A metal roofing material wraps the house to protect it. (South elevation) *Thomas McConnell@ mconnellphoto.net*

95

The homeowner required an exterior ramp to rise the 20 feet to the house. A poured concrete walkway rises from the covered parking area below. *Thomas McConnell@ mconnellphoto.net*

Part of the original design program was a ramp in place of stairs to reach the house. The exterior switchback ramp allows for a gentler ascent or descent. *Thomas McConnell@mconnellphoto.net*

The west elevation shows a rigid frame shape and covered parking area below for cars, as well as boat storage. *Thomas McConnell@ mconnellphoto.net*

Lit at dusk, the house is a jewel box with its exposed interior and metal framework. Today, it is a point of reference for boaters on the lake. The raised portion of the roof houses the second floor's master bedroom suite and home office. *Thomas McConnell@mconnellphoto.net*

Ten-foot wide covered porches, created by the rigid frame and the elevated concrete platform, are oriented to take advantage of the best lake views and capture the breezes off the water. The wide space is ideal for entertaining outdoors, even on hot Texas summer days. *Thomas McConnell@mconnellphoto.net*

The public spaces of the house are flooded with natural light, and well connected to the surrounding covered porch. *Thomas McConnell@mconnellphoto.net*

Upper East River View

On the upper East Side of Manhattan, this colorful modern living room designed by Vanessa Deleon Associates engages the East River view. *Courtesy of Dan Muro, fastforwardunlimited*

The inviting dining room has a contemporary style. *Courtesy of Dan Muro, fastforwardunlimited*

Dark accent cabinets and a dynamic patterned ceramic mosaic backsplash give this kitchen a special motif. *Courtesy of Dan Muro, fastforwardunlimited*

The family room has clean lines and minimalist style. *Courtesy of Dan Muro, fastforwardunlimited*

The refreshing workspace has colorful accents and a great view of the upper East Side. *Courtesy of Dan Muro, fastforwardunlimited*

The bedroom has a full view of the East River. *Courtesy of Dan Muro, fastforwardunlimited*

A touch of glamour marks the modern bathroom. *Courtesy of Dan Muro, fastforwardunlimited*

California Beachfront Condo

For this Seahaus beachfront condominium located in La Jolla, California, Ami Samuel Interiors incorporated a neutral yet high contrast color palette along with contemporary furniture and beach-themed accessories to give the illusion of bringing the beach indoors. *Courtesy of Ami Samuel Interiors*

Texas Coast Condo

The entry corridor needed to pull attention away from the spectacular bay view and become a space of its own. The undulating stick ceiling adds interest while hiding low ductwork that crosses the entry hall. The dark blue on the wall was selected to show several black and white prints and drawings and compliments the pieces with color as well. *Courtesy of Chris Cooper*

The clients wanted to begin the experience of their collection outside their front door but in a safe environment. So the design team from M & J Larcade commissioned four different inlaid glass mosaic panels with a flower garden motif created by Erin Adams. This floor installation, set into the same black porcelain tile used throughout the condominium, can be seen from the kitchen and breakfast table through the windows on the right. *Courtesy of Chris Cooper*

The angled wall in the living room created space for a small alcove for the clients' metal sculpture that will not fade in direct sunlight. *Courtesy of Chris Cooper*

The clients wanted a clean contemporary space with low maintenance and casual living, yet one that would exhibit their art collection well. They loved color, which is reflected throughout by both their art selections and how the pieces are displayed. The long side of the condominium opens to a balcony overlooking the bay, which floods all the rooms with light. By creating the diagonal wall at the far end of the living room, the space expands and opens the view towards the city, most apparent at night with the city's lights. The floors throughout are black porcelain tile. *Courtesy of Chris Cooper*

Another view of the living room has the beginning of the curved wall leading to the dining room on the right. White on the walls has both the sculptural effect of the curves and showcases a very colorful and intricate nine-piece painting. *Courtesy of Chris Cooper*

The serpentine wall leads to the dining room on the right and to the exercise room at the far end. It was designed to activate and break up the long rectangular footprint of the condominium. *Courtesy of Chris Cooper*

The dining room is on the interior side of the condo with no windows or natural light, so the decision was to make it a dramatic space. The client had commissioned Dale Chihuly to create a special wall piece for the room. To focus the attention on the Chihuly wall, M & J Larcade covered the cabinets on either side in a dark inlaid wood and the remaining walls upholstered a rich brown fabric. The black granite table reflects the glass colors in its surface. The chairs are upholstered in four jewel tones to further enliven the space along with the red Tibetan rug. *Courtesy of Chris Cooper*

The powder room off the entry gallery is painted a soft mottled white. A deep blue glass basin, which appears candy colored and luminous, sits in a black granite counter top. The mirror on the wall is framed with clusters of hand blown glass flowers in both clear and white glass. *Courtesy of Chris Cooper*

The clients' favorite color is orange. Since color relationships are part of the fun, M & J Larcade used hot and cool colors, which are then viewed with the blue of a kitchen wall and the entry corridor and a painting beyond. *Courtesy of Chris Cooper*

The media room is painted all red to diminish the brilliant light coming off the water and to work with the hand hooked rug, part of the clients' thirty-year collection. Cabinets are Brazilian rosewood. The bridge tabletops are also Brazilian rosewood, but the legs are stained black similar to the floors. Vertical blinds can be pulled over the window wall to darken the room for better television viewing. *Courtesy of Chris Cooper*

Ami Samuel Interiors used a seaside color palette of blues, chocolate brown, and neutrals along with contemporary design elements to give this Mission Bay condo a great open and inviting beach feel. *Courtesy of Ami Samuel Interiors*

House on the River

FORMA Design transformed the subdued entry doorway of this riverside house with a splash of celadon. *Courtesy of Geoffrey Hodgon Photography*

The white concrete fireplace with the flat screen TV attached commands the center of the visual axis, while the indigo blue wall creates a dramatic backdrop. The custom Cha-Cha rug is from FORMAonline.com. The simplicity of the furniture selection against this backdrop helps create a comfortable *Zen* feeling. *Courtesy of Geoffrey Hodgon Photography*

The white artichoke pendant light creates a dramatic centerpiece floating above the glass and steel dining room table off the open kitchen and breakfast bar. The open plan encompasses the kitchen, living and dining areas, all sharing the sunlight pouring in from all directions, while allowing for the river views to be shared from every angle. Light bamboo floors reflect the sunshine coming in from all directions. A minimally dropped ceiling defines the kitchen work area. *Courtesy of Geoffrey Hodgon Photography*

The stone fireplace surround with the hanging flat screen monitor become the focal point of the family room with comfortable loungers that allow for long movie viewing in comfort. The study/guest bedroom lies beyond the sun-dried tomato wall with the pocket doors. *Courtesy of Geoffrey Hodgon Photography*

The custom sun-dried tomato Cha-Cha rug from FORMAonline.com helps define the sitting area of this master bedroom suite, with uninterrupted views of the Potomac. Chaises flank a wenge wood long cocktail table, on axis with the custom TV wall and the floating audio/visual cabinet. *Courtesy of Geoffrey Hodgon Photography*

The pebbled floor plays up the views of the river below. Glass partitions separate the shower and toilet compartments from the main bathing area, while sharing the sunlight streaming in. Playful cutouts in the privacy film separate the private from the semi-private areas. *Courtesy of Geoffrey Hodgon Photography*

The custom floating millwork and concrete countertops help support the floating "his" and "hers" mirrors in this master bath facing the river. The sandblasted glass sheets have some areas mirrored and some clear areas. This technique permits the sunlight to stream in during the day, while always providing for a mirrored surface for shaving or brushing. *Courtesy of Geoffrey Hodgon Photography*

Pennsylvania Log Home on a Pond

Rill Architects designed a new custom home on the 200-acre farmland to replicate an old log house. Overlooking a private 20-acre pond, the home is built with a series of buildings creating outdoor rooms to take advantage of the scenic water and wooded views. Local stone used inside and out as well as natural logs and lots of glass reflect a well-thought out plan for this weekend retreat. *Courtesy of James Ray Spahn*

Authenticity comes to life in this stone and timber office with a new stone fireplace designed to feel like it had been there for years. Influenced by historic precedence, this space offers period lighting, beamed and vaulted ceiling, and expanses of glass, including French doors that open to the incredible surroundings. *Courtesy of James Ray Spahn*

Rill Architects surrounded the home with plenty of flagstone patios accented with boulders and stone indigenous to the site. A stone fireplace completes the setting made for outdoor entertaining. *Courtesy of James Ray Spahn*

Simulating an enclosed porch with exposed rafters, the dining room is surrounded by wood-framed windows and water views. With seating for 10 plus, the indoor eating area complements the outdoor banquet-size spaces. *Courtesy of James Ray Spahn*

Homeowners and guests relish being one with nature on this property while relaxing on this flagstone patio with rustic seating. *Courtesy of James Ray Spahn*

115

California Beachside

The client at this beachside residence located in Encinitas, California, requested a transitional design scheme from Ami Samuel Interiors, which incorporated traditional elements with a clean contemporary look in the living, family, and dining room areas. The use of floor-to-ceiling paneled walls, rich dark wood flooring and warm color scheme are examples of the traditional elements along with the more contemporary hand-painted ceiling, furniture, lighting, and accessories that were used in the living and dining room. *Courtesy of Ami Samuel Interiors*

The family room with its blue and neutral color palette, track lighting, mix of traditional with contemporary furniture pieces and accessories complete the transitional look for this beachside homeowner. *Courtesy of Ami Samuel Interiors*

Severn River Retreat

Situated about 30 feet from the Severn River at the foot of a cliff, this small Maryland retreat designed by Rill Architects is approximately 800 square feet. *Courtesy of Timothy Bell Photography*

Two entryways flank the fireplace in the living room and lead to a 20 x 35 square-foot glass room with space for dining and game tables. The glass room was once the screened-in porch. *Courtesy of Timothy Bell Photography*

The dark wood island that doubles as a table takes center stage in this utilitarian kitchen. White wood walls and cabinets plus limestone tiles finish the roomy cooking space. *Courtesy of Timothy Bell Photography*

Two bedrooms on one side of the home open to the great room and inviting kitchen with vaulted ceilings. *Courtesy of Timothy Bell Photography*

This one-story home features two bedrooms including this owners' suite. Windows are positioned to optimize views. *Courtesy of Timothy Bell Photography*

Shenandoah River Valley Retreat

A series of terracing decks links the exterior spaces on the western side of this house designed by Carter + Burton Architecture. The kitchen inside is connected to the "summer kitchen" outside, up to the screen porch, and down to the chemical-free spa as an intermediate node. The butterfly roof control sun and water from impacting the interior of the house. *Courtesy of David Afzal*

The master bedroom on the eastern wing of the house sits lightly on sonotube foundations to allow ground water to pass back to feed the river below. *Courtesy of David Afzal*

After a full day kayaking on the river, the owners and their friends come back to the deck wrapping the western side of the house. The exterior grill center and screen porch create a "summer kitchen." This is essential in keeping extra heat out of the house in Virginia's hot, humid summers. *Courtesy of David Afzal*

The breathtaking view of the Shenandoah River Valley disappears when approaching this retreat house and then appears again from the inside. A floating formal entrance separates the private bedroom wing from the public living wing. The concrete tower highlighted in the center of the house, reminiscent of fire lookouts in the surrounding mountains, serves as an exhaust for rising hot air in the summer through operable windows, while providing a bird's eye view of the river below. The SIPs roof panels provide an elegant profile never before available with such a high level of insulation and structural durability. *Courtesy of David Afzal*

Minimal furnishings are aided by custom built-in storage along the north wall. The latter buffers the home from northern storms and displays sliding art panels hiding closets, cabinets, and shoe storage almost the entire length of the house, framing the treetops through the windows above. The high cool north light mixes with the warm southern light for balanced daylighting. The fireplace is made from Heatcrete, a more durable material suitable for high temperatures. *Courtesy of David Afzal*

The aesthetic of the owner is to provide a minimalist foreground in which to enjoy nature through the windows beyond. The inhabitant becomes directly engaged with the view of the sparkle on the river at the built-in dining table and benches made from stabilized aluminum foam (100% recyclable and non-combustible). The exposed concrete floor and the cantilevered concrete office balcony above warm in the winter sun and slowly release this heat into the open plan in the evenings. This radiant heat is critical to energy efficiency as it is keeping the heat down low where the furniture and people are rather than warming air, which will rise to the high ceiling. *Courtesy of David Afzal*

After an afternoon exploring the Shenandoah River's fish and wildlife, guests can escape the sun in the cave-like, bermed in lower level lounge, which opens completely to the lower patio area. This blending of inside and outside heightens the experience with nature. *Courtesy of David Afzal*

South Beach Retreat

In this beach apartment for an out-of-town owner in Miami's chic South Beach, white is the predominant color, letting the eye focus on the blue sea beyond. Accessories and artwork are the only splashes of color throughout the apartment. *Courtesy of Geoffrey Hodgon Photography*

As night falls, the blue LED light matches the blue of the South Beach sky, which becomes an evocative backdrop to this simple yet stylish apartment, designed by FORMA Design. *Courtesy of Geoffrey Hodgon Photography*

The white-on-white theme continues in the selection of the dining table and chairs as well as the buffet, the artwork and the accessories in this South Beach pad. The kitchen beyond features under counter stainless steel appliances and an elaborate Rococo mirror that allows views of the guests while the owner is cooking. *Courtesy of Geoffrey Hodgon Photography*

The kitchen for this South Beach pad for an out-of-town owner is compact yet functional. All appliances, including the double drawer refrigerators, are under the counter, letting the space feel much bigger than it actually is. The back wall, the only one with upper cabinets, is dressed in a local stone, while the left wall features an elaborate Rococo mirror reflecting the artwork on the opposite wall. *Courtesy of Geoffrey Hodgon Photography*

In this hallway to the private rooms, the mid-century modern white paneling, blue LED lighting cove, white on white stone flooring and furniture allow for the "Angel I" photograph (from AndreasCharalambous.com) at the end of the axis to shine. *Courtesy of Geoffrey Hodgon Photography*

In the guest bathroom, the porcelain walls and flooring, the toilet and vanity as well as the back painted glass top of the bathroom cabinet, all in white, play up the contrast to the wenge freestanding cabinet and square framed mirror. The sandblasted glass paneled door allows for natural light to enter unobstructed. *Courtesy of Geoffrey Hodgon Photography*

The magnificent Miami skyline beyond the bay acts as a dramatic backdrop to this elegantly simple bedroom. Here the white palette of the finishes and furniture is broken only by the brown of the wenge king size bed and pillows and the orange cover and artwork.
Courtesy of Geoffrey Hodgon Photography

Beachfront Condo

In this contemporary beachfront Seahaus condominium in La Jolla, California, Ami Samuel Interiors used a neutral color palette with a splash of a bold color such as red, contemporary furniture, lighting, accessories, and beautiful eco-friendly cork flooring to bring a warm and inviting space to life. *Courtesy of Ami Samuel Interiors*

Hover House

The simple concept of a box hovering over the garden level addresses the constraints of this 32 x 95 foot lot on the canals of Venice. The structure hovers above the small lot enabling a truly useful garden scale. Such a tight site doesn't encourage bold departures from the "box" without exacting huge compromises on the inhabitants, so Glen Irani embraced the box. This "box" is an open-ended square tube with a canal-facing façade strategized to aim views, create privacy, and express the luminescent and colorful spirit of the interior. A huge pivoting steel and glass window overhangs the facade line, offering another example of the technical expertise with which this precision box was designed and built. Exterior artificial slate panels modulate the exterior scale and facade features. *Courtesy of Derek Rath Photography*

At the top of the exterior stair, one arrives at the entrance terrace where, in powerful contrast to the grey monotone exterior, finish details energize the space and signal visitors to enter the colorfully appointed interior. Immediately ahead, a custom fabricated frameless glass sliding door opens to a compressed corridor space flanked by the main interior stair shaft. *Courtesy of Derek Rath Photography*

The outdoor living area is, without a doubt, the heart of the house. Outfitted with a fully appointed kitchen including refrigerator, icemaker, dish drawer, sink, cook top and BBQ, this garden-level space is great for entertaining. A solid walnut dining island, heated concrete pavement, waterproof walnut cabinet fascias and a sandblasted concrete block fireplace round out the finishes for a feeling of connection to the natural world without detracting from the cool, machine-like aesthetic of the building. *Courtesy of Derek Rath Photography*

Natural light floods this "water space" through louver-protected frosted glass. The architect really wanted the master bathroom to express the precision and attention to detail commensurate with, but at a more tactile level than the exterior architecture. Custom fabricated single-side finished polymer paneling and cabinetry doors add depth, luminescence, and precision to the surfacing while the architect's custom Corian 2-fer lavatory and coupled stainless steel wall-mounted faucets bring the husband and wife together, if only for a few moments when days get too busy. Basalt stone countertop, stainless steel trim, and heated concrete floors round out the finishes. *Courtesy of Derek Rath Photography*

A two-story flight of scissoring steel-plate stair treads mounts to a center wall of thick clear glass hung from the ceiling of the stair shaft by two steel bars. By flooding the shaft with daylight, the brilliant orange-red painted surfaces create a luminescent sense of arrival and punctuation to the entry area as well as an exhilarating experience when transitioning to the upper levels. *Courtesy of Derek Rath Photography*

Tropical Waterfront Townhouse

The third floor has a tempered clear glass stairway landing with a frosted border. The blue vaulted ceiling reflects the sky and the sea. *Courtesy of Victor Elias/VPL Photo*

The split level entrance of this townhouse remodeled by Jerry Jacobs has 20–foot limestone (Crema Maya) columns capped with double cross vaults, a Hemisphere pendant light, and a split-level balcony. Local limestone is used in the floor tiles and wall flush baseboards. The arched hallway leads to the living room and the garden beyond. *Courtesy of Victor Elias/VPL Photo*

The main wall of the living-dining area is mirrored to reflect the East Bay water view. The fabric on the pillows is Cowtan & Tout and Osborne & Little. The elliptical buffet is by Century, and there is a linear HVAC diffuser. *Courtesy of Victor Elias/VPL Photo*

The master bedroom has a mirrored back wall. Notice the shower portholes. The bed is reflected in the back mirror. The sitting area fabric is Manuel Canova. *Courtesy of Victor Elias/VPL Photo*

The full 30-foot length windows join the bed and the sitting area. The spa has a vanishing edge on two sides, an outside bench to rotate from, and a ficus tree encircled by steps. *Courtesy of Victor Elias/VPL Photo*

This bedroom has bright blue walls, an arch, and a reflected ceiling. *Courtesy of Victor Elias/VPL Photo*

Assawoman Bay Deckhouse

Two-homes-in-one defines this unique deckhouse overlooking the Assawoman Bay leading to Delaware and Maryland beaches. Designed by Rill Architects, the home includes panoramic 180-degree views of the water via glass corners and multi-level decks. *Courtesy of Timothy Bell Photography*

The two structures shown from the water replace a 1960s rambler and detached garage. The larger 3,500-square-foot structure is the guesthouse with five bedrooms. The main house is about 1,800 square feet with three bedrooms. *Courtesy of Timothy Bell Photography*

Exposed exterior rafters give composition and rhythm to the interconnected homes, which are a work of art. *Courtesy of Timothy Bell Photography*

Floor-to-ceiling windows and wood from top to bottom give the guesthouse's living room a rustic and relaxed feel. *Courtesy of Timothy Bell Photography*

Half wood, half glass, one of the three main house bedrooms offers just enough privacy while also providing a vantage point to overlook the Assawoman Bay. *Courtesy of Timothy Bell Photography*

Wire railings, mimicking those found on boats, work both inside and outside this deckhouse designed by Rill Architects. Wood paneling is the perfect complement to a busy household. *Courtesy of Timothy Bell Photography*

Island Flair

High wooden columns provide a grand entrance to this tropically designed game room. The home, located in Southern California, causes a person feel they are on an island in the tropics. The unique focal point to this space is the outrigger placed high above the pool table. The designer, Kathy Abell of Designed Interiors, with the help of the Outrigger Club in Waikiki, Hawaii, designed the craft to incorporate lighting. Created by a custom furniture maker, the outrigger is made the finest wood. Woven wood blinds bring in warm, natural lighting and the large pieces of tropical artwork balance the space. *Courtesy of Cogdell Photography*

A spiral staircase leads up to a master suite that's designed to have the feel of a tropical plantation. Natural woven wood blinds bring in natural light, and lush surroundings are viewed through tall, duel paned windows. In addition to the deep wood finishes, the unique tropical artwork brings color to the space. The raised hearth fireplace, framed beautifully in wood, creates an inviting and relaxing atmosphere. *Courtesy of Cogdell Photography*

An additional view of the master suite shows the romantic canopied bed, rattan furniture and beautiful periwinkle blue fabrics. A French door leads to the master bath on the left; on the right, a second set of French doors lead to the second story balcony. The room has a spa feel that invites one to relax and unwind. *Courtesy of Cogdell Photography*

Upper East Side

This 3,500 square feet residence is located in upper East Side Manhattan, close to East River. The view from 34th floor terrace and the floor-to ceiling-windows stretches north and east over the river and its bridges far to Queens and Brooklyn. The tone of the residence is inspired by the surrounding city, air, and water below. Warm silver and foggy grays as well as deep browns in many textures dominate Magdalena Keck's palette. The living room features a large sectional sofa in gray linen and a round dark wood coffee table. The floor is finished with large- scale honed Richmond Gray limestone and softened by a wool rug by Christopher Farr. Works on paper are by Amanda Guest. *Courtesy of Jeff Cate*

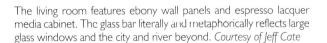

The living room features ebony wall panels and espresso lacquer media cabinet. The glass bar literally and metaphorically reflects large glass windows and the city and river beyond. *Courtesy of Jeff Cate*

Magdalena selected warmer tones for the kitchen. Stainless steel appliances and thick stainless steel counter top complement cabinets in espresso lacquer. The Richmond gray limestone floor stretches throughout all the public spaces of the entire apartment including the kitchen. *Courtesy of Jeff Cate*

The designer's goal was to visually enlarge the powder room space. Vertical cove lighting was created. The main wall features a full height mirror and mini brick matte nickel tiles. *Courtesy of Jeff Cate*

The master bathroom features a wall-mounted vanity with vessel sinks. Above the vanity a full height mirror reflects a custom mosaic with image of tree branches. The mosaic wraps around the bathtub enclosure and continues up the wall into the light cove. *Courtesy of Jeff Cate*

The master bedroom's walls are painted very dark brown, almost charcoal color. The lacquer credenza is in the same color. Fully upholstered wall acts as a headboard. Silk carpet completes the room. Floor-to-ceiling windows on north side offer exquisite views of the city and Central Park. *Courtesy of Jeff Cate*

Magdalena injected purple and magenta tones in the children's room to complement the silver grays present throughout the apartment. The main feature is a custom "cat" wallpaper with deep purple background. The white and polished aluminum simple desk almost disappears in front of the window. The Eames aluminum group desk chair is upholstered with magenta hopsack fabric. There are also two sculptural elements: purple beanbag and a long fringe pendent lamp that drops almost to the floor. *Courtesy of Jeff Cate*

The guest bedroom is done in tones of foggy gray and dark deep brown. Geometric shapes of the custom night table and the floor lamp are contrasted with the softness of black and white photography. *Courtesy of Jeff Cate*

4.
Mediterranean

"Where are our castles now, where are our towers"? lamented Sir Thomas More (1478-1535). Today, we can find them in many beautiful places: from mountaintops to cities, from sparkling waterfront to verdant valleys. Here are those Mediterranean houses that lie on the water's edge.

Courtesy of Linda Williamson Photography

Courtesy of Eleanor Lund

145

Lakeside Villa

The approach and entrance feature breathtaking views of the lake and hills that surround the home. *Courtesy of Coles Hairston Photography*

The trickling sound of a fountain invites you into the cozy entry court of this Italianate lakeside retreat. The owners' desired a private, cloistered retreat that could also be used to entertain large groups. They turned to Vanguard Studio. Inc. *Courtesy of Coles Hairston Photography*

A groin-vaulted gallery welcomes visitors and contributes to creating a special, intimately scaled and elegant passage that pulls you out to the lake. *Courtesy of Coles Hairston Photography*

The bold arches echo throughout the house – not only in the wall openings, but also in the ceilings. *Courtesy of Coles Hairston Photography*

The clients required a state-of-the-art kitchen for entertaining that also has the same attention to architectural detailing as the rest of the home. *Courtesy of Coles Hairston Photography*

The main outdoor living areas are large enough to accommodate a crowd and sit literally on top of the lake. *Courtesy of Coles Hairston Photography*

The main family room has a picturesque connection to the lake. *Courtesy of Coles Hairston Photography*

The soaring family room focuses on the two-story fireplace adorned with a relief of the "god of wind." *Courtesy of Coles Hairston Photography*

The master bedroom has a breathtaking view of the lake. *Courtesy of Coles Hairston Photography*

The master bath and its tiled soaking tub "with a view" are spectacular. *Courtesy of Coles Hairston Photography*

Point Pleasant

The clean lines of this exterior entry create a modern take on the Mediterranean style that is finely tuned by the warm tones of the stucco and added accent of the tile work framing the store and doors. *Courtesy of Tim Proctor & Associates*

The numbered tiles displaying the address are imported European tiles, which were hand picked by the designer: Vanessa DeLeon Associates. *Courtesy of Tim Proctor & Associates*

This uncluttered entry sets the tone for the Mediterranean styled house. Also setting a masculine tone are the oversized candleholders and vase that help to balance the wagon wheel effect that the beams form on the ceiling above. The natural wood accents that surround the circular foyer give an old world feeling to the grand entrance. *Courtesy of Tim Proctor & Associates*

The use of tile and wrought iron details balance the curved wall of windows allowing light to brighten this rustic entry. The one-of-a-kind chandelier lantern accentuates the dome ceiling and rustic wood beams. *Courtesy of Tim Proctor & Associates*

Vanessa DeLeon Associates created a warm inviting place to entertain when she mixed antique elements with more modern pieces in this living room. A classic mantel and artwork frame a modern marble fireplace. *Courtesy of Tim Proctor & Associates*

The potter tile base topped with the copper vessel sink and deep orange walls makes this additional powder room exude a rustic quality while fitting in with the Mediterranean style of the house. The cracked stone tile that borders the floor of the bathroom is also paired with the clean seamless mirror. *Courtesy of Tim Proctor & Associates*

This seating area showcases the client's taste incorporating a couch that was from a previous house and combining it with a mix of modern pieces. The open feeling created by the positioning of the furniture and use of space throughout the room gives a comfortable openness to this living area. *Courtesy of Tim Proctor & Associates*

A modernized classic arcade separates the dining area from the living room. The use of these columns was a perfect way to capitalize on the Mediterranean feel of the home and designate areas simultaneously. Because the columns have arches between them rather than a wall, they help maintain an open feeling. *Courtesy of Tim Proctor & Associates*

When entering this modern, masculine master bedroom the eye is immediately drawn to the custom tiled fireplace. The double view fireplace also separates the sleeping area and sitting area in the master suite. *Courtesy of Tim Proctor & Associates*

With earthy tones and natural light, this guest bedroom makes for a perfect place to retreat after a busy day at the beach. *Courtesy of Tim Proctor & Associates*

The master bathroom exudes masculinity with the crisp angles, which are accented by the balance of slate tiles and the blue of the walls. The louvered windows add an element of natural light. The custom built wood shutters give a Mediterranean feel and enhance the bathroom design. Adding a bit of warmth to this bathroom is an inviting wood double vanity topped with fixtures. The concrete countertop compliments the slate tiles, but the leather finish gives it a cleaner softer touch. *Courtesy of Tim Proctor & Associates*

Villa Montaña

Designed by Vanguard Studio, this home is a classic blend of hacienda, hill country, and Italian stone styling. Great for entertaining, the residence boasts stunning lake views and a pool. Once inside, a rich juxtaposition between refined elegance and embracing warmth bring the senses alive in the open, airy home. *Courtesy of Coles Hairston Photography*

Visitors enter the loggia just to the left of the entry. A light and bright transitional area, it has the feeling of an old, enclosed porch with its pecky cypress ceiling and limestone pilasters. Iron French lanterns and sconces light the large area as it overlooks an upper courtyard through large multi-pane windows. *Courtesy of Coles Hairston Photography*

While the layout is very open, overlooks and columns throughout the house create private areas and niches. *Courtesy of Coles Hairston Photography*

The open family room focuses on capturing the incredible views. One of the room's walls is a sliding glass door that disappears when opened and leads out onto the massive veranda. Best of all, there is a glass railing so none of the view is obstructed.
Courtesy of Coles Hairston Photography

Unique materials that help it create its own sense of coziness mark the kitchen. Rosewood cabinets, rainforest granite, and mesquite floors link the house to the nature preserve that surrounds it.
Courtesy of Coles Hairston Photography

High quality light fixtures and sconces give the house a beautiful glow, particularly through the radiant stained glass window in the stairway. *Courtesy of Coles Hairston Photography*

A panoramic view of Lake Travis is a focal point for both master bedroom and bath (upper right). Rich fabrics, a subtle color palette, and period and contemporary furnishings complement the view. *Courtesy of Coles Hairston Photography*

Jersey Shore Tuscany

Diane Boyer Interiors, LLC worked closely with the clients during the construction of their new three-story beach home. Like many seashore residences, the main living quarters are located on the upper floors to take advantage of the sweeping shoreline views. *Courtesy of From House to Home/Jonathan Harper*

The open and curvaceous staircase graces the ground floor entryway, which also houses a multi-passenger elevator for easy transition between floors. The first floor contains two bedrooms and a sitting room; the second level includes the kitchen, dining, and living spaces; and on the third floor, there is a TV room. *Courtesy of From House to Home/Jonathan Harper*

The designer's attention to detail extends to every room in this space, from multiple powder rooms and bathrooms to mini-bars on the first and third levels. *Courtesy of From House to Home/Jonathan Harper*

This guest bedroom has its own balcony, as do the other three bedrooms in the home. *Courtesy of From House to Home/Jonathan Harper*

The master bath and spa incorporate a mix of limestone and ceramic tile.
Courtesy of From House to Home/Jonathan Harper

Limestone tiles, in varying sizes, add interest and texture to the spaces. With two small children, the client desired a balance between a formal house and an easy-to-maintain beach house. Durango stone (a natural stone consisting of marble, limestone, and high quality travertine) was used on the first floor. Imported limestone was used on the second. The stone textures add warmth to the decor and are easy to care for. *Courtesy of From House to Home/Jonathan Harper*

The large kitchen island, equipped with wine rack and icemaker, provides ample space for cooking and casual dining. *Courtesy of From House to Home/Jonathan Harper*

The first-level guest suite includes a sitting room. Its furnishings are upholstered in durable combinations of fabric and leather to withstand the effects of sun and sand. *Courtesy of From House to Home/Jonathan Harper*

With proximity to Atlantic City making this home a year-round destination, the custom fireplace and entertainment center are a focal point of the second floor's open plan. *Courtesy of From House to Home/Jonathan Harper*

The wife's wish for a bit of Tuscany at the Jersey shore is reflected in the soft color palette and rustic stone and plaster treatments, both real and faux, throughout the spaces. An arched wall defines the dining and living spaces. *Courtesy of From House to Home/Jonathan Harper*

Generous decks off the main living level, as well as balconies off the third floor bedrooms and a patio off the ground floor guest suite, provide sweeping views of the distant skyline. *Courtesy of From House to Home/Jonathan Harper*

In the dining room, the transition from a limestone to a wood floor, as well as the hand-painted cove ceiling, immediately marks this as a more formal space. The window treatments are sculpted valances with string panels called "Cordon" by Ado. *Courtesy of From House to Home/Jonathan Harper*

Villa Comanche

The client, a restaurateur, interior designer, gallery owner, art collector, and land developer, asked Vanguard Associates for an under-stated European facade with a dynamic and fluid interior. The result was a residence that rests gently on a sloping lot facing the lake and its beautiful views. The plan is oriented to allow as many rooms as possible to enjoy unobstructed views from both levels and the large outdoor living area. The front of the building has limited openings and allows the imagination to wonder what lies behind the stone and stucco exterior. Beyond the entry tower lies a small courtyard, which allows natural light into the foyer and dining room and allows glimpses of the sculptural stone staircase inside the house. Interior detailing and materials make this home both modern and timeless.

The resulting eclectic mix of materials, detailing, and styles combines to create a rich tapestry, an old world estate. *Courtesy of Coles Hairston Photography*

The entry tower features a custom gate and old world sconces that evoke a sense of mystery. *Courtesy of Coles Hairston Photography*

The actual entry gate hints at the interior courtyard beyond.
Courtesy of Coles Hairston Photography

Immediately upon entering the home, you are drawn to a spiral staircase with a unique brass railing that is reminiscent of an old castle stair. *Courtesy of Coles Hairston Photography*

The curved stone staircase sweeps the visitor upstairs. Classic details like arches, groins, and vaults – even in the bedroom – echo the fluidity of the entry stair. *Courtesy of Coles Hairston Photography*

Vanguard's design called for a variety of natural stone, including limestone, sandstone, and granite for both interior and exterior elements. This element provides warmth and texture throughout the home and brings coziness to the elegant atmosphere. *Courtesy of Coles Hairston Photography*

A balcony with a detailed iron railing overlooks the formal dining room. *Courtesy of Coles Hairston Photography*

The focal point of the master bath is the serene soaking tub set beneath a large arched window that connects you to the lake beyond. *Courtesy of Coles Hairston Photography*

The soaring outdoor living room allows for expansive views of the lake beyond.
Courtesy of Coles Hairston Photography

5.
Classic

Courtesy of D. Peter Lund

Courtesy of D. Peter Lund

Isle of Wight Home

In the 1960s, the clients bought a late 1800s home on the south shore of Long Island. Later they decided to purchase the equally old house next door to use as a guest home. In 1984, Charlene Keogh of Keogh Design, Inc., was hired, along with Bill Taylor of Taylor Brothers Construction, to oversee the renovation and to make necessary upgrades to the interior and exterior of the guesthouse. In 1989, the architect, Chris Schmitt of Schmitt Walker Architects was hired to design a new home to replace the existing home. Schmitt designed a house that complimented the existing guesthouse and yet stood on its own with a craftsman/shingle style architecture that enhanced the adjacent house and other older houses in the neighborhood. This view shows both houses with the pool house. Grasses surround the pool structure. *Courtesy of Dan Muro, fastforwardunlimited*

In 2003, the clients wanted to add a pool and develop privacy landscaping, linking the two houses together. Hank White of HM White Site Architects joined the team for the landscaping effort. Hank White developed a comprehensive site and landscape plan that reconciled the many environmental regulatory requirements while addressing surrounding property privacy edge conditions, wetland, and adjacent tidal marsh habitats and satisfying a set of client use needs. A series of landscape design principles emerged that improved the sense of separation between the guest and main house while revealing the unique qualities of the property's upland wetland forest habitat. The entry courtyard links the two homes and pool area. *Courtesy of Dan Muro, fastforwardunlimited*

Both houses with hot tub and lap pool are seen here. *Courtesy of Dan Muro, fastforwardunlimited*

View from dock back to houses. *Courtesy of Dan Muro, fastforwardunlimited*

This view of pool and yard area looks out to a channel and then to the Atlantic Ocean. *Courtesy of Dan Muro, fastforwardunlimited*

The main house has a curved screened porch that opens onto the generous backyard with its orchard and salt marsh beyond. *Courtesy of Dan Muro, fastforwardunlimited*

The new rounded screened porch was added during the final phase of the project. *Courtesy of Dan Muro, fastforwardunlimited*

The living room of the main house contains an antique wicker chair with a Kilim rug and an early twentieth century Japanese tea hibachi, modified for a coffee table.
The full height French doors open fully to the screened porch. *Courtesy of Michael Keel Photography*

The center element of the house is a massive fireplace that opens onto the living room on one side and the dining room on the other. The open relationship of these two spaces, and how they open onto the screened porches, makes the house ideal for entertaining. Randy Taplin in Warren, Vermont, designed and built the Stickley style dining room table and chairs. The Japanese screen is from the late nineteenth century. *Courtesy of Michael Keel Photography*

To one side of the dining room is a spacious kitchen and breakfast area that also opens onto the screened porches. This kitchen was designed to also accommodate catering for parties and dinners. *Courtesy of Michael Keel Photography*

At the top of the stairs on the second floor is a balcony area that serves as the client's library. *Courtesy of Michael Keel Photography*

In the master bath, custom tiles are interspersed in the floor design.
Courtesy of Michael Keel Photography

The colorful master bedroom boasts art storage in wood flat files (see lower left) and Kabuki Japanese dolls in the glass case. Keogh Design created the custom headboard and side tables. *Courtesy of Michael Keel Photography*

This view shows the front of the guesthouse with the courtyard.
Courtesy of Dan Muro, fastforwardunlimited

The guesthouse has a linked pool and deck.
Courtesy of Dan Muro, fastforwardunlimited

In the guesthouse living room, a new fireplace surround was created to match details on the windrow and door moldings. *Courtesy of Michael Keel Photography*

In the guesthouse dining room, new doors open to the screened porch and the pool beyond. The Charles Rennie Mackintosh high back dining chairs and round table provide "a room within a room." New corner display cabinets were added to balance the existing corner fireplace in the living room. *Courtesy of Michael Keel Photography*

Connecticut River Conservatory

George Fellner of Fellner Associates Architects designed this conservatory addition to a house on a bluff overlooking the Connecticut River. The 240 square foot southwest-facing addition to a 1930s 4,700 square foot home was designed to create a visual dialogue with the river. Nestled between dual gables, the new shed/half octagon form is a logical resolution of the program requirements. Paying homage to the existing home's Tudor style, the integrated expansion serves to enhance the picturesque quality of the architecture and its waterfront site. *Courtesy of George Fellner*

A conscious effort was made to allow the new materials to complement the existing facade. In a sense, the new stone base appears to grow out of the adjacent walls, embracing the new form. The new stone embedded stucco face with half-timbering relates to the adjacent gables. Initially cascading from the steep gable, the new slate shed roof evolves into a radial pattern. Furthermore, the new copper gutters and leaders accommodate the rainwater from the various roof planes. All in all, the materials offer a sustainable solution with virtually no required maintenance or replacement. *Courtesy of George Fellner*

Serving as an extension of the circulation path connecting the great room with the master bedroom, the new conservatory offers an intimate space for relaxing and socializing. The open ceiling serves as a direct response to the roof geometry, celebrated as a sculptural form. The multi-directional, low-E double glazed windows provide generous views up and down the river, as well as to the pastoral fields. Additionally, they accommodate both natural daylighting and ventilation. A closed-cell spray polyurethane foam insulation system provides R-21 in the walls and R-37 in the roof. 2-in. extruded polystyrene board insulation provides R-10 below the concrete slab. A geothermal system efficiently accommodates the heating and cooling requirements. Furthermore, the rotating double fans help to circulate the air during all seasons. *Courtesy of George Fellner*

Duxbury Waterfront Residence

This large, year-round home overlooking Duxbury harbor has a Federal-style exterior with a completely reconfigured interior layout. The main rooms have harbor views, and those on the lower floor have fireplaces. The natural light enhances the monochrome color palettes that harmonize with the natural tones of water and sky. The owners are able to step from the interior to screened-in porches on both floors. Jerry Rippetoe of tj's at the Sign of the Goose uses a medley of similar hues for a peaceful setting that allows the special views and furnishings to shine. *Courtesy of W. Garrett Scholes*

The rectangular layout is cut in the center to create two conversation areas with ocean views and access to a screened in porch. Gold-colored wall coverings and a pale blue ceiling reflect the light of the sea. *Courtesy of W. Garrett Scholes*

This room sees a lot of entertaining. Bright water views illuminate the blue wallpaper and blue ceiling in the day. The client's Venetian chandelier sparkles in the bright daylight and creates a wonderful mood at night. *Courtesy of W. Garrett Scholes*

This tiny space offers a tranquil spot for television and music. Again, a door opens to a screened porch, and shades of rich blue color circle the walls, floors and ceiling. *Courtesy of W. Garrett Scholes*

The client wanted to wake up looking at the water. Thus, the bed "floats" in the space, allowing the client to wake up looking at the ocean. Soft green color envelopes the room — the wide stripe wall covering, the window treatments, and ceiling. *Courtesy of W. Garrett Scholes*

Mid-century Update

A bowling alley-shaped 1940s ranch house in Washington's San Juan Islands attracted its new owners with panoramic saltwater views and sunrises over the majestic Cascade Mountains. Interior designer Molly McIntosh of Gracious Living Interior Design assisted the couple with reconfiguring a maze of small rooms to incorporate expansive vistas while creating a warm yet spacious setting for year-round retirement living. To enhance the feeling of the space, the ceiling was raised to roof level and gracious moldings, cove lighting, and gently curving lines were added. Furnishings and accessories incorporate carefully layered classic details blended with warm colors and subtle rich textures, giving the once-cramped ranch the feeling of upscale casual elegance. *Courtesy of www.kp-studios.com*

A broad open stairway with two-story windows facing the water (out of view to the right) separates the relaxed family room from the more upscale living room. Here, more casual traditional furnishings are paired with quilted fabrics, soft colors, buffalo check curtains, and a leather sofa to define a casual space for everyday living. The two-toned coffee table ties together the room's blend of wood and painted elements while echoing the adjacent living room's golden hues. Custom cabinetry by Canyon Creek Cabinet Company provides a stage for the owners' to tell their personal story.

Accordion doors open fully to make the room one with the deck, terrace, and bay, with its ongoing parade of sailboats, yachts, and whale-watch and commercial fishing boats. *Courtesy of www.kp-studios.com*

The total renovation of the 1940s ranch removed a wall to open the kitchen to the rest of the open living area and the home's expansive water views. McIntosh worked with Canyon Creek Cabinet Company on the cabinetry design for the kitchen. The kitchen echoes the soothing soft teals and subtle textures of the adjacent family room. Cream-colored cabinetry is accented by a sea foam island, softly colored granite countertops, marble mosaic tiles on the range hood and island backsplash, and an artichoke motif behind the cooktop – suggesting the local valley's abundant produce. Natural wood floors add warmth and flow from kitchen to family room. The window cornice repeats the family room curtain fabric, tying the two rooms together and injecting a subtle splash of color and pattern.

To suggest the home's retro origins, subway tiles were used behind the counters and a furniture-like look applied to the custom cabinetry through distressed finish, inset door panels, and nickel bin pulls. A second small sink on the island helps with vegetable prep, clean up, or use as a bar. *Courtesy of Scott W. Thompson*

Soothing tones in the master bedroom carry through the home's golden and teal hues. Classic detailing is applied subtly to create an uncluttered look. Sophisticated custom bedding, designed by McIntosh, uses chocolate fringe on bed pillows to add a dash of drama to the room. The elegant yet restful retreat shares the home's eastern exposure, with a wall of windows to take in morning traffic on the waterfront. Throughout the project, Gracious Living worked with the home's owners to incorporate an existing art collection and favorite accessories into the reconfigured structure and all-new furnishings and fixtures. *Courtesy of www.kp-studios.com*

Elegant paneling, a granite fireplace surround, and sumptuous furnishings lend an upscale feel to the traditionally styled, below-grade den. Concrete floors were acid-stained a rich dark brown, then warmed further with elegant oriental rugs. McIntosh increased the harmonious feel by carrying the windowsill trim into the chair rail. The accent appears to embrace the space. *Courtesy of Canyon Creek Cabinet Company*

Handsome built-in drawers in the lower-level home office give file cabinets a good name. Tropical brown granite makes a durable and stylish top for counters and desk. The built-in peninsula desk projects from a custom alder wood wall with abundant space for storage, books, and display. *Courtesy of Canyon Creek Cabinet Company*

Seaside Bedroom

The sweeping Atlantic Ocean views outside this gracious Queen Anne style family home were among the inspirations for the designer, Mary Strout. Several shades of watery blues and creams envelope this bedroom and serve to continue the serene atmosphere of a pleasant day at the beach. A delightful use of printed and textured fabrics and an eclectic mix of discovered sea treasures create a not too serious approach to this timeless bedroom. Inherited pieces are given a new life with attention to details, such as contrasting piping along the pillow edges and skirts. Seaside paintings are a gentle reminder of summer days. *Photo © Eric Roth*

Courtesy of D. Peter Lund

Once a boathouse in the center of the village, it is now a little, but well loved, house that hangs out over the water. The visitor enters a room filled with family heirlooms and antiques. *Courtesy of D. Peter Lund*

The interior has a contemporary appearance with its continuous flow of space and the intermingling of the exterior and the interior, while the details are traditional: family paintings, fireplace appliances, and a piano in the corner. *Courtesy of D. Peter Lund*

From the porch or from the inside of the house, the residents and their fortunate guests can observe the busy bay. *Courtesy of D. Peter Lund*

St. Michael's Farm

Stately, restrained and purposeful, the rhythm of doors and windows on the land side of this farm c. 1805 masks a rich history of growth, change, and adaptation that unfolds within and which is only apparent from the water's edge. Alt Breeding Schwarz Architects was the architect, and Dawson Begley Designs was the interior designer for the 2005 restoration. *Courtesy of LydiaCutter.com*

Although both the 1805 and 1850 wings have formal entries of their own, a new enclosed breezeway functions as the daily family entry at the new center of the farm: the crossroads of family gathering and outdoor water sports, hunting and entertaining by the pool and on the dock. Simple massing, beautiful proportioning, and faithful detailing of materials gracefully meld the new additions to the historic core of the house. *Courtesy of LydiaCutter.com*

Ebonized doors and a darkly painted glossy ceiling (in Drab, by Farrow & Ball) dramatically focus one's attention on the water beyond. The pedestal table, a richly carved English Regency antique made in 1815, was purchased and moved from the Bank of England and then moved to new premises, for the first time since the early nineteenth century. This farm is its second home. *Courtesy of LydiaCutter.com*

Original paint fragments found on the fireplace surround inspired rich red colors in the textiles. Maps of the Chesapeake Region and Hogarth prints of the period echo eighteenth century life. The original plaster ceiling's decayed state provided an opportunity to remove it to show the original floor joist carpentry and pegging above. Both the wife and the designer lived and studied in Williamsburg; this room is a tribute to their experience with colonial traditions. The wooden hayforks were a house-warming present from the designer to the owners to commemorate their new life as the couple from the painting "American Gothic." But with better clothes! *Courtesy of LydiaCutter.com*

Opening onto the brick-paved pergola, the living room is surrounded by old boxwoods and a sweep of lawn running toward the water. The owner's furnishings were repurposed for this room, united by a coordinating rug and new Swedish and English antiques. *Courtesy of LydiaCutter.com*

The kitchen commands the center not only of the house but also of the 17 acres that serve as the home place within the larger farm. Sight lines to every part of the farm are possible from the kitchen's work island. The approach of guests from the land, returning fishermen, boaters and jet skiers from the dock, people lazing at any of three outdoor entertainment areas, or in the family room adjacent, or the lawn beyond are all visible from this vantage point, this new center of farm life.

To create a strong identity for this room, a strong dark red color anchors the space, and a low-walled banquette creates enclosure while capturing water views for this interior room. Reclaimed first-growth Heart Pine floors glow and reflect the unusual light of this neck of land jutting out into the Chesapeake Bay as well as continue the historic house flooring into this new wing seamlessly. *Courtesy of LydiaCutter.com*

For much of the nineteenth century, arriving at the farm was much easier by water than by land. The source of much of the room's furnishings; India; Africa; France; England, and The West Indies tell the story of trade along the Bay and the source of wealth and goods for those living by it. *Courtesy of LydiaCutter.com*

A custom computer, storage and work center anchors the family roof, echoing the coloration of the solid rosewood Indian bench used as a coffee table. Expansive doors opening onto the lawn frame 270-degree views of water, a formal boxwood and cutting garden, farm fields and woods beyond. Approaching storms are magical from this vantage point as the waterside alcove is fully glazed. Curtains on a continuous rod across this 22-foot opening allow light control and insulation when the house is not occupied. *Courtesy of LydiaCutter.com*

The additions of a closet to one side and a bathroom to the other resulted in another window placement design challenge. Here, window panels are stacked behind the bed as a full-height ground for the client's sleigh bed, thereby preserving views of both the Farm and The Bay. The Cowtan & Tout panel fabric and collected shells and watercolor drawings are reminders of the client's great love of St. Barth's and the Caribbean Sea. *Courtesy of LydiaCutter.com*

Londonderry Designer Show House

The historic property known as Londonderry in Easton, Maryland, exemplifies the 1860s Gothic Revival style crafted by Richard Upjohn. Sailing, views of the Tred Avon River and a relaxed lifestyle within this region provide refuge to families from Washington, D.C. to New York City. Brad Weesner was among the designers who brought the home back to life via the Londonderry Designer Show House, which benefited The Historical Society of Talbot County.

The 14-foot ceilings and narrow dimensions of the room called for a large backless bench crafted after an original piece at the Winterthur Home in Pennsylvania. The oversized bench and silk pillows create a place to nap during the day and entertain at night. Clean lines and edited accessories work with the room's Neo-Classic elements and allow Kevin Fitzgerald's "Evening Pond" oil on canvas to take center stage. The calming artwork reflects the theme of the room, which changes colors and moods in different light.
Courtesy of Geoffrey Hodgdon

Bringing together old and new, this corner of the room showcases Greg Horwitch's "The Three Ages of Man" oil on canvas that combines the classicism of an Old Masters work with surprise elements such as the Rubik's Cube by a contemporary artist trained at the Florence Academy of Art. The bench is finished with a pewter-cut velvet and black lacquer legs for a modern twist. The table is custom by Brad Weesner Design. *Courtesy of Geoffrey Hodgdon*

On this side of the room, both corners hold symmetrical displays of Italian Demi-lune tables and mirrors with open fretwork, while the contemporary lamps add a component of modernism. The Neo-Classic lines are again pared down for today's aesthetic. Other finishes include Scott de Montluzin's "Parthenon Detail," graphite on paper showing depth and realism, and a Baker chair. *Courtesy of Geoffrey Hodgdon*

6.
Resources

Alt Breeding Schwarz LLC doesn't just design beautiful homes, they orchestrate them. Beginning with the client's "score"—their needs, budget, and aesthetic goals—the firm synthesizes a complex tapestry, marshalling creative responses to unique site opportunities and zoning constraints, eliciting and polishing strong design concepts and expressive architectural forms, researching environmentally sustainable technologies as well as materials that are historically fitting, and sifting and testing textures, colors, and details. The firm has been orchestrating beautiful homes in the Chesapeake Bay region for over 25 years.

> 209 Main Street
> Annapolis, MD 21401
> 410.268.1213
> web: www.absarchitects.com
> email: sb@absarchitects.com

Known for its unique style and exclusive client attention, **Ami Samuel Interiors (ASI)** is emerging as one of Southern California's most sought after design firms. For more than five years, ASI has been translating design trends and concepts into tangible award-winning experiences (2007 SAM Awards Winner). The common characteristic in ASI's residential and model home projects is a perfect balance between style and substance. The success of ASI can be attributed to the strength of its design vision — "atmosphere is everything."

> 11211 Sorrento Valley Road, Suite Y
> San Diego, CA 92121
> 858.453.9789
> web: www.amisamuelinteriors.com

Bennett Howard Studio provides interior design services for commercial and residential projects throughout Seattle and western Washington.

> 5342 Rockaway Beach Road NE
> Bainbridge Island, WA

Brad Weesner Design's mantra, "beauty creates beauty," coupled with the designer's holistic approach to interiors produce spaces that lighten spirits and make the world a more beautiful place. The firm listens to clients' wishes and incorporates lighting, color, and furnishings to create calming environments for upscale residential homes, hospitality clients and restaurants, and corporate interiors. Brad Weesner has a strong background in home building, architecture, and landscape design that enables his firm to work seamlessly with professionals in those fields.

> Everedy Square,
> 6 N. East Street, Suite 100
> Frederick, MD 21701
> 301.631.0990
> web: www.bradweesnerdesign.com

Carter+Burton Architecture P.L.C. is a small Virginia architecture firm that specializes in a few good projects per year. Located in Berryville, a small town one hour west of Washington, D.C., its architects enjoy designing and working within a wide range of budgets. The firm's focus is on quality, craftsmanship, and innovation. It tries to promote passive solar techniques and eco-friendly building materials.

> 11 W. Main Street
> Berryville, VA 22611
> 540.955.1644
> web: www.carterburton.com
> email: jim@carterburton.com

Chester Architecture LLC is dedicated to two simple philosophies: 1. "Design Matters." Design creates the image, comfort and functionality of the spaces we live, work, and play in daily. 2. "Design is Fun." The design process should be one of the most enjoyable processes that architectural clients can have.

> 120 Madrone Lane, North Suite 201
> Bainbridge Island, WA 98110
> 206.842.1775
> email: bill@chestercarroll.com

2010 marks the twentieth anniversary of **Dawson Begley Design's** London founding. Its work is based upon ancient principles of solid construction, refined spatial relationships and fine proportions, and detailing to create classic, elegant, and timeless settings for life. The firm is particularly adept at working on site and within budget and at designing in real time to maximize construction efficiency. Employing the latest building system technologies, sustainability principles, and both local expertise and a worldwide network of artisans and resources, the firm's timeless approach to room making creates living environments of lasting value. Typically, Dawson Begley Design's projects are built to stand for 400 years and are landmark expressions of home and hospitality in their communities.

> 1000 Potomac Street NW, Suite 202
> Washington, DC 20007
> 202.338.7365
> web: www.dawsonbegley.com
> email: jdb@dawsonbegley.com

Diane Boyer, ASID is the owner of **Diane Boyer Interiors, LLC**. Her design firm is noted for its ability to handle large-scale residential projects – those in the 6,000 to 30,000 square foot category with luxurious amenities. She received multiple Design Excellence awards from the New Jersey Chapter of the American Society of Interior Designers, including three gold awards. Her work has appeared in a wide range of national and regional publications.

> 271 Grove Ave., Bldg. C
> Verona, NJ 07044
> 973.857.5900
> web: www.dianeboyerinteriors.com
> email: design@dianeboyerinteriors.com

Designed Interiors is an interior design firm in San Diego County specializing in residential and commercial interior design. Its designers, owner Kathy Abell, Joan O'Haver, and Terese Moser have over 46 combined years' experience in the design field. Since 1990, Designed Interiors has had the privilege of designing versatile projects throughout San Diego, as well as clients' vacation homes in Lake Tahoe and Hamilton, Montana. The firm's desire is to let the client's unique expression and personality shine through all projects, whether large or small. *San Diego Home/Gardens Lifestyle Magazine* and *Better Homes and Gardens Magazine* have featured the work of the firm.

> 10180 Quail Canyon Road
> El Cajon, CA 92021

Michael Ferzoco is the president and founder of **Eleven Interiors**, a talented team of designers who creates sophisticated spaces unique to each client. Featured on a cover of *Design New England Magazine*, the firm is also the recipient of the 2009 PRISM Award for Best Interior Design-Living Space, awarded by the Builders Association of Greater Boston. The firm has consistently garnered regional and national recognition and has been featured in a number of publications including *Elle Décor, Boston Common Magazine, TRENDS, Boston Spirit Magazine,* and the *Sunday Boston Globe Magazine*.

> 535 Albany Street, 4th level
> Boston, MA 02118
> 617.423.1114
> web: www.eleveninteriors.com
> email: michael@ eleveninteriors.com

Fellner Associates Architects (FAA) is committed to the development of responsive architectural solutions. Founded in 1987, FAA has designed building types that include banquet and conference centers, municipal, community, health care, recreational, commercial, and residential projects. In order to produce responsive architectural solutions, the juxtaposition of context, semantics, sustainability, and pragmatics is sensitively balanced. As Co-Chairman of the AIA Connecticut Committee on the Environment, George Fellner, AIA, LEED AP, is responsible for developing programs and workshops related to sustainability including alternative technologies and materials.

> 415 Killingworth Rd.
> Higganum, CT 06441
> 860.345.7558
> web: www. fellnerarchitects.com
> email: fellnerarchitects@sbcglobal.net

Established in 1994, **FORMA Design**'s multi-disciplinary approach results in high quality, concept-driven design solutions that efficiently and effectively maximize the client's time and financial resources. It has received numerous local, regional, and national awards; been published extensively in a number of publications, and featured on TV. Andre Charalambous, AIA, IIDA, Principal, combines over twenty years of experience in architecture and interior architecture with his deep interest in all aspects of design and a career in painting and photography.

> 1524 U Street, NW, Ste 2
> Washington, DC
> 202.265.2625
> web: www.formaonline.com
> email: mail@formaonline.com

Glen Irani, Principal of **Glen Irani Architects**, developed his knowledge of highly exclusive contemporary residential design during his employment at the studio of John Lautner FAIA, and later at Richard Meier and Partners. In 1994, he began his own practice with a focus on contemporary residential, commercial, and cultural projects for clients who are committed to creating unique contemporary environments that respond to their lives as well as the physical and cultural context in which they reside. The work of Glen Irani Architects has been widely exhibited and published worldwide.

> 410 Sherman Canal
> Venice, CA 90291
> 310.305.8840 or 310.822.1801
> web: www.glenirani.com

Molly McIntosh, NWSID, ASID Allied Member, is the owner of **Gracious Living Interior Design**®, offering a full range of home design services for upscale clients in the Pacific Northwest. Her gracious, warm, and inspired environments have received numerous awards and recognitions, and her projects are regularly sought after for home tours and publications. She is listed in International *Who's Who in Interior Design*™ and *Who's Who in America*™.

> P.O. Box 1079
> Anacortes, WA 98221
> 360.299.8949
> web: www.graciouslivinginteriors.com

HM White Site Architects is founded on the principle that the designed landscape is among the most powerful forms of cultural expression. Founded in 1992, the firm prides itself on creating high performance and multi-function landscapes that are rooted in sustaining a site's natural systems and fulfilling its user's needs and aspirations. Through HM White's award-winning and celebrated work, clients and communities have come to expect landscapes with consistent clarity of vision that are site-specific, artful, compassionate, timeless, and ultimately enhance life.

> 130 West 29th Street, 9th Floor
> New York, NY 10001
> 212.868.9411
> web: www.hmwhitesa.com

A small design-oriented architecture firm, **James D. LaRue Architects'** talented and diverse professionals have brought their experience, education, and interests to a design-intensive environment. The firm focuses on creating residences that are custom, responsive, and sustainable. Its clients will find that the design process is very interactive and practical, while remaining highly creative, versatile, and site sensitive.

With over 400 residences and offices completed, James D. LaRue Architects brings extensive experience and expertise to every project.

> 614 S. Capital of Texas Highway
> Austin, TX 78746
> 512.347.1688
> web: www.larue-architects.com
> email: kil@larue-architects.com

Jerry Jacobs Design offers interior design and architectural design services in the San Francisco Bay Area. Its work is featured in many publications, including *Architectural Digest, House Beautiful, Objekt, Shelter Interiors,* and *Vogue*. Whether it's a pied-a-terre, a townhouse, or an oceanfront vacation home, the firm creates distinctive and functional design solutions for discerning clients in San Francisco and throughout the United States and Mexico. Jerry Jacobs Design has completed numerous projects including private residences and villas, apartments, boutiques, clubs, and lobbies.

> 169 Stewart Drive
> Tiburon, CA 94920
> 415. 435.0520
> web: www.jerryjacobsdesign.com

Founded in 1983 by Judd Brown and Steve McMahon, **Judd Brown Designs** (JBD) has successfully completed an impressive array of design projects for both hospitality and residential clients. A staff of more than 25 design professionals has created a multitude of award-winning interior and exterior designs throughout the world. Together, with their sister-architectural firm, Jefferson Group Architects led by Wayne Jacques, AIA, NCARB, LeedAP, JBD continues to provide highly creative and complete design solutions for satisfied clients throughout the United States.

> 700 School Street
> Pawtucket, RI 02860
> 401.721.0977
> web: www.jbd.cc

Keogh Design, Inc., founded in 1988 by Charlene Bank Keogh, ASID, CID, is best known for high-end residential interiors tailored to each individual client. Timeless, unique furniture and product designs are a hallmark of the firm, which has design projects throughout the United States. Ms. Keogh has received AIA's Excellence in Interiors Award and brings to her clients a lively mix of creativity, passion, and fun in combination with a pragmatic business approach. The firm's work has been featured in numerous publications, including *Interior Design, Design Times,* and *Dwell* magazines and *Spectacular Small Kitchens: Design Ideas for Urban Spaces; Retreats to Retirement:*

Dream Homes to Reality; Contemporary Kitchens: A Style Portfolio; and *Asian Influence on Architecture and Design* (Schiffer Publishing).

180 Duane Street
New York, NY 10013
212.964.4170
web: www.keoghdesign.com

Kingsley Belcher Knauss ASID (KBK), ASID, with over twenty years of experience, provides interior design solutions to residential and commercial projects. Her design philosophy stresses a close link between the disciplines of architecture and interior decoration. KBK has the expertise to create a wide variety of interior environments from traditional to contemporary. Her firm strives to develop interior environments with an underlying classicism that survives the passage of design trends.

205 Benson Place
Westfield, NJ 07090
908.789.2831
email: info@kbkinteriordesign.com

John and Margaret Larcade are owners of **Larcade Larcade, Architecture, Interior Design and Color.** Their firm handles small to medium residential and commercial projects. They are known for a great deal of personal attention and their dedication to details. John has been involved in historic preservation and contemporary projects in New York, Texas, and Mexico. Margaret has received an IBD award for product design, is known for her color work, and also worked on contemporary projects in New York, Texas, and Mexico.

511 East Craig Place
San Antonio, TX 78212
210.733.0260
web: www.larcadelarcade.com
email: margaret@ larcadelarcade.com & john@ larcadelarcade.com

Magdalena Keck has been creating residential and commercial interiors for nearly a decade. Keck's streamlined designs have been published in *Interior Design, VM+SD,* and *Kitchen and Bath News.* She has been featured among 40 established and up coming New York designers in the book *Spectacular Homes of Metro New York* (January 2008). Keck's current residential work includes high-end residences in New York and Miami and renovation of a Frank Lloyd Wright Usonian house in Westchester County, New York. Inspired by nature, art, and technology, Keck's signature approach combines immaculate craftsmanship and function to achieve a distinctive elegance through honest, clean, and genuine design.

12 West 27th St., 10th Floor
New York, NY 10001
212.725.7704
web: www.magdalenakeck.com
email: mkeck@ magdalenakeck.com

Mary Donnellan Strout Interiors is known for timeless and comfortable homes. Mary's personal touch with each project creates living spaces that are warm, inviting, and unique to each client. She offers a wealth of knowledge from her extensive educational background and professional experience in the decorative arts, period antiques, and historical homes and gardens. Mary believes that rooms should tell a story and look well traveled. They should reflect who lives in the home, what their passions are and where they have been.

235 Elm Street
East Longmeadow, MA 01028
413.530.0290

Celebrating 25 years as an architect, James F. Rill AIA of **Rill Architects** has dedicated himself to designing picturesque-style, environmentally friendly residential homes in the Washington, D.C. area. As one of the only residential architectural firms in the region truly using a three-dimensional design process, Rill Architects can give homeowners an accurate depiction of the final design and its relative cost early in the design process. Rill Architects listens to the homeowners' wishes, realizing they, as architects, are just visitors to the home and site; the owners are the ones living there. The cohesive Rill Architects' team includes architects Linda Gallegos, Kay Kim, James Murray, and Richard Rossi and office manager Tom DiMisa.

4833 Rugby Avenue, Suite 501
Bethesda, MD 20814
301.656.4166
web: www.rillarchitects.com.

Ruth Richards Interiors, a branch of Interiors at Woodside LLC, is committed to providing detailed custom designs, personalized to each client's individual needs, budgets, lifestyle, and preferences. Ruth is known for her beautiful and timeless, yet eclectic interiors that show an interesting diversity in design styles. Ruth believes that a perfect balance in color, pattern, texture, materials, objects, and nature is essential to every room. Her passion for nature extends to the exterior of the home as she has an incredible gift for garden design as well.

973.763.2645
web: www.ruthrichardsinteriors.com

Established in 1986, **Schmitt Walker Architects** has been honored with numerous national and regional design awards. Its projects have received extensive coverage in various professional and consumer publications. The firm's design philosophy is based upon appropriateness of design to context, directness, economy of means, and careful tailoring of the architectural expression to the client's expressed requirements. Most of the firm's projects have been produced within tightly managed budgets, while the firm's work has been widely recognized as innovative and eloquent.

12A Vanderhorst Street
Charleston, SC 29403
843.727.3140
web: www.schmittwaler.com

Swift-Morris Interiors' commissions have ranged from Caribbean villas to urban brownstones, and design projects in between. Carol Swift's style is always original and innovative, using color and unique palettes as distinctive elements in each interior. Her approach to interior design integrates her clients' lifestyle with an assured aesthetic sensibility and an appreciation for fine furnishings and art. She has created indelible rooms in ten major designer showhouses along the eastern seaboard. Her tasteful and innovative work has graced the cover of *New York Spaces*, and has been featured in *Southern New England Home* and *New England Home* magazines.

1208 Washington Street
Hoboken, New Jersey 07030
201.656.5684

69 Mill Street
Newport, RI 02840
401.849.3229
web: www.SwiftMorrisInteriors.com

Taylor Brothers Construction has been in existence since 1976. Its primary business of building new homes or renovating existing homes occurs in and on the south shore of Long Island: Lawrence, Atlantic Beach, Long Beach, and Point Lookout. Its services run from small additions, bathrooms, and kitchens to multi million dollar renovations. It develops long-term relationships with its clients, who become friends.

32 Malone Avenue,
East Atlantic Beach
Long Island, NY 11561
516.889.9282

Teal Michel ASID provides symmetry, detailing, and quality of products. She creates remarkable interior spaces that speak to their owners. A native of the Northeast, her work is cosmopolitan yet comfortably livable. Her trademark is impeccable style and professionalism in every project she designs — big or small.

3736 Surry Ridge Ct.
Charlotte, NC 28210
704.554.7036
web: www.tealmichelasid.com
email: tealmichel@juno.com

The hallmark of **tj's at the Sign of the Goose** is an unapologetic use of the finest quality materials that transforms a residence into an experience both memorable and practical. Jerry Rippentoe, who masterminds its interior design services, draws on a wealth of resources, including artisans, custom furniture makers, and highly experienced installers. His experience and talent are reflected in his personal credo of "Good Design is Forever." His clients agree — with many having him design multiple residences. His sense of great design and great quality results in places of distinction as well as repose.

1287 Route One
Cape Neddick, ME 03902
207.363.5673
web: www.tjsgoose.com
email: info@tjsgoose.com

Vanessa DeLeon Associates is an award-winning design firm. Vanessa DeLeon, ASID Allied member, specializes in high-end residential, commercial, and hospitality interiors. Her work has been featured in over two dozen national and regional publications. Hall of Fame Jamie Drake honored her as one of three rising stars of 2007. A frequent personality on HGTV, she was on the first season of Design Star and several other shows.

934.5 River Road
Edgewater, NJ 07020
201.224.9060
web: www.vanessadeleon.com

Since its creation in 2000, **Vanguard Studio, Inc**., has been creating award-winning homes that are warm and inviting, yet have an aesthetic refinement that their clients require. The firm's belief in the timelessness of extraordinary architecture is evident in its use of the elegant contours and lines of Italian and Spanish structures from the past. Ensuring that their client's vision is fully realized is a priority for the firm's principal architect, John Hathaway. "We believe strong design that is responsive to the client's needs and dreams is always possible," he says, "no matter what constraints exist." The firm uses its experienced team, innovative technology, and professional integrity to provide its clients with a broad range of options and ideas to suit every taste.

6601 Vaught Ranch Road, G-10
Austin, TX 78730
512.918.8312
web: www.VanguardStudio.com
email: John@VanguardStudio.com

Strongly emphasizing integration of site and structure, **Webber + Studio** strives to link indoor and outdoor zones. The results produce buildings and spaces that take on the unique characteristics of each site and client. Since 1997, Webber + Studio, located in Austin, Texas, has brought this sensibility to all of their projects, whether residential, commercial, or institutional. The firm pursues projects of varying type, scale, and use in an effort to constantly hone our skills and philosophy so that we may always bring the highest level of quality and value to each of our endeavors.

300 West Avenue, Suite 1322
Austin, TX 78701
512.236.1032
web: www.webberstudio.com

Other Resources

I was fortunate enough to know several talented photographers who gave me some additional images:

Lydia Cutter Photography is a fine art photographer with an impressive list of commercial clients. She works in the DC area, traveling to clients in Arizona, Utah, California, New Mexico, and Colorado.

5953 Woodacre Court
McLean, VA 22101
703.625.2015
web: www.LydiaCutterPhoto.com
email: Lydia@ LydiaCutterPhoto.com

Jim Somers has been making photographic images for over 30 years. Finding images is a refinement of something he has done for years — wandering the fields and woods near his home for things of interest. He will see a color, or a line, or several components juxtaposed, and move around until he finds the image by fitting the pieces into a rectangle. Water, with its intense and abstracted reflections, and ice, with its surprising lines and depth, are his current favorite subjects. His work appears in juried art shows in New York and New Jersey.

33 McKinley Ave
West Caldwell NJ 07006
web: www.somersphoto.com
email: jimsomers@mindspring.com

Linda Williamson has had a love and a fascination for the beauty of the world. Growing up in the historic, picturesque town of Concord, Massachusetts, and traveling to many places, has added to this allure. Photography has enabled her to document and share her passion. She can only hope that you, the viewer, find the same passion for her work as she does. "Beyond beauty there is truth in every photograph."

Westford, MA 01886
978.846.0414